TABLE OF CONTENTS

TABLE OF CONTENTS (Continued)

CHAPTER 1

INTRODUCTION

> Your fellow citizens think they have a right to
> full information, in a case of such great
> concernment to them. It is their sweat which is to
> earn all the expenses of the war, and their blood
> which is to flow in expiation of the causes of it.
> Thomas Jefferson, January 26, 1799.[1]

The purpose of this study is to discuss the historical factors which form the basis for past U.S. wartime press censorship and what significance these factors have on future U.S. military operations. This introduction contains the study's assumptions and pertinent definitions. Succeeding chapters discuss wartime press censorship from the Colonial era through Vietnam. The final chapter contains a discussion of the effects of technology on future wartime press censorship.

This study is based on several assumptions. The first assumption is that some form of press censorship has been used in past U.S. conflicts. Secondly, there are social and legal objections to press censorship in the U.S. which originate from a strong legacy of press freedom.

Thirdly, the U.S. armed forces depend upon an informed, supportive American public for the legal authority to exist, funds to operate, manpower, and materials. And finally, technological change makes it impossible to restrict the flow of information from future battlefields.

This thesis will examine, in light of the assumptions listed above, what is the historical background of U.S. wartime press censorship and what form, if any, future wartime press censorship by U.S. military commanders should take.

Definitions

Throughout this paper, *censorship* is considered either prior restraint, censorship at the source prior to publication, or the imposition of such stringent restrictions on the publication of information on U.S. military operations as to be in fact prior restraint.

In the U.S. military the *Field Press Wartime Information Security Program* (also referred to in the U.S. Joint Operations Planning System as Field Press Censorship)[2] is a formal Department of Defense program of "security review of news material subject to the jurisdiction of the Armed Forces of the United States, including all information or material intended for dissemination to the public."[3] The program was officially eliminated in 1987.[4] No procedures have been implemented to replace it.

A second pertinent definition is the term *accreditation*. For the purposes of this study, accreditation is formal recognition of a media

representative by a U.S. commander in a theater of

operations. Media representatives will be referred to as

correspondents in this study, meaning:

> A journalist, press reporter, photographer,
> columnist, editor, publisher, radio or television
> reporter, commentator, cameraman, newsreel or other
> documentary picture production employee accredited
> to the Department of Defense and regularly engaged
> in the collection and dissemination of news to the
> public.[5]

The term *ground rules* means guidelines on

information agreed to by military and media representatives

which may be used when reporting on the operations of U.S.

armed forces in combat.

A final definition is the *National Media Pool*. The

pool is a twelve-person team representing U.S. media that

deploys to areas of operations overseas to provide news

coverage of Department of Defense operations. The pool

normally deploys representatives of both print and

broadcast media to areas not otherwise accessible to the

media. Pool news products are provided to other national

and local media as a condition of the pool agreement.

CHAPTER 1 ENDNOTES

1. Thomas Jefferson to Elbridge Gerry, 26 January 1799, *The Writings of Thomas Jefferson*, Thomas Jefferson Memorial Association, Washington, 1904, Vol 10, p. 83.

2. Joint Chiefs of Staff, *The Joint Operation Planning System—Volume I Deliberate Planning Procedures (SM362-84)*, Washington, D.C., 1984, p. F-16.

3. U.S. Department of Defense, *Wartime Information Security Program (WISP) (Department of Defense Directive 5230.7)*, Washington, D.C., with changes through 21 May 1971, p. 3.

4. U.S. Department of Defense, Defense Department Directives System Transmittal Cancellation Notice for Department of Defense Directive 5230.7, "Wartime Information Security Program (WISP)," Washington, D.C., 21 January 1987.

5. U.S. Department of the Army, Department of the Navy, Department of the Air Force, *Public Information: Establishment and Conduct of Field Press Censorship in Combat Areas (Army Regulation 360-65, Operational Naval Instruction 5530.3A, Air Force Regulation 190-11)*, Washington, D.C., 1966, p. 2.

CHAPTER 2

U.S. WARTIME PRESS CENSORSHIP'S COLONIAL HERITAGE

The legal basis for U.S. wartime press censorship has an English heritage. During America's colonial period, English printers were required to present their material to the government before publication. Censors arbitrarily approved, deleted or changed the material. In addition, printers were licensed by the government. Without a license, printing was forbidden.[1] Material on the armed forces was not excepted. An Act of Parliament in 1649 "provided that the Secretary of the Army would be empowered to license all army news."[2]

"Treason" and "sedition" were the initial targets of the legal efforts of censors in England during America's colonial period. The punishment for these or any other capitol offense was unbelievably harsh in modern context. An English writer convicted of sedition in 1633, William Prynn, was sentenced to be pilloried, to a 10,000 pound fine, to life imprisonment, and to have his ears cropped off.[3] John Twynn, convicted of treason for printing a book critical of the government, received the following sentence:

> . . . that you be . . . drawn upon a hurdle
> [sledge] to the place of execution; and there you
> shall be hanged by the neck, and being alive, shall
> be cut down, and your privy-members shall be cut
> off, your entrails shall be taken out of your body,
> and you living, the same to be burnt before your
> eyes; your head to be cut off, your body to be
> divided to four quarters . . . And the Lord have
> mercy on your soul.[4]

This heritage of control of the press and harsh punishment

for offensive writing accompanied English colonists to

America.

The publication of what is believed to be the first

newspaper in the colonies was ended after one issue due to

the colonial government's desire to control publication of

military information. Benjamin Harris printed the *Publick*

Occurrences in Boston in September 1690. The paper

described in some detail the defeat of a small colonial

force by a body of French and Indians in the Massachusetts

colony earlier that month. Despite the rather mild,

uncritical tone of the account, the perceived criticism of

the handling of the operation drew an immediate reaction

from the government:

> Immediately on its publication it was noticed
> by the legislative authorities. Four days after,
> they spoke of it as a pamphlet; stated that it came
> out contrary to law, and contained ˙reflections of
> a very high nature.˙ They strictly forbade
> ˙anything in print, without license first obtained
> from those appointed by the government to grant the
> same.˙[5]

Though there ˙was nothing very offensive in any of

the intelligence˙ that appeared in the paper, the

legislature was ˙peculiarly sensitive to any infringement

of their power.° This issue of *Publick Occurrences* was the first and last newspaper published in the colonies until 1704.°

In May 1722, New England was startled by the appearance of a small pirate ship off Block Island, near Newport, Rhode Island. The ship conducted a series of attacks on shipping along the New England coast. Word of the attacks reached the Massachusetts House of Representatives on June 7th. On June 8th, the House commissioned a ship to hunt down the pirates, with the vessel to be ready for sea on June 11th.[7] The *New England Courant* wrote that day,

> We are advised from Boston, that the Government of the Massachusetts are fitting out a Ship, to go after the Pirates, to be commanded by Captain Peter Papillon, and 'tis thought that he will sail some time this Month, wind and weather permitting.°

This caustic comment on the slowness of the military response landed Benjamin Franklin's older brother James, the *Courant's* printer, in prison. In what was probably the second attempt to control the publishing in America of military information, James Franklin was jailed by the Massachusetts colonial government for more than a month.°

Franklin obtained his release by petitioning the government:

> In Council, 20th June, 1722, a petition of James Franklyn, printer, humbly shewing that he is truly sensible and heartily sorry for the offence he has given to this court in the late *Courant*, relating

to the fitting out of a ship by the government, and truly acknowledges his inadvertency and folly therein in affronting the government, as also his indiscretion and indecency when before the court, all which he intreats the court's forgiveness, and praying a discharge from the stone prison where he is confined by order of the court.[10]

Colonial government control of the press through the licensing of printers also resulted in an order to Franklin preventing him from printing or publishing the *Courant* or any Pamphlet or paper of the like Nature, Except it be first Supervised, by the Secretary of the Province."[11] Though Franklin evaded the order by substituting brother Benjamin's name on the paper, a ruse which allowed him to continue publishing, the tone of the *Courant* became more subdued.

The *Courant* case was followed by another colonial order declaring that

> . . . the printers of the newspapers in Boston be ordered upon their peril not to insert in their prints anything of the public affairs of this province relative to the war without the order of the government.[12]

Until shortly before the Revolution, while political commentary repeatedly resulted in fines, imprisonment, or arrests for violating censorship edicts, military commentary was rarely so outspoken as to tempt the colonial governments into taking printers to court. There was therefore little military censorship by the colonial governments. But as the rift between Colonial America and England widened, abusive, inflammatory rhetoric appeared in the colonial press. When the patriot press openly spoke of rebellion, Tory mobs and British troops destroyed several newspapers. Patriot mobs in turn attacked and destroyed the presses of several printers who professed neutrality or were openly loyalist.[13]

Censorship in the Revolution

During the Revolution, loyalist and patriot mob action was augmented by political censorship by the patriots' new state governments.[14] This political censorship was limited to censoring dissent. Though state governments repeatedly used their authority to quash political dissent,[15] they made little attempt to censor war news. This was caused in part by the haphazard reporting of the war in the revolutionary press. War news was not gathered by correspondents who directly observed the war, rather, any report of the war, any official or semi-official message from the colonial government or British forces, even private letters, were published. The 'papers of the Revolutionary period took their news as it drifted in.'[16] The delay this caused in the publishing of news on operations concerning both sides, from a week to more than a month,[17] removed some of the impetus to punish violations of the censorship edicts.

Another force preventing punishment of censorship violations was the reluctance of the Continental Congress to take action. Though General George Washington wrote to Congress in 1777:

> It is much to be wished that our printers were more discreet in many of their publications or accounts transmitted by the enemy of an injurious nature. If some hint or caution could be given them on the subject, it might be of material service.[18]

no effort at censorship was made.

One explanation for this reluctance is the founding fathers' dedication to freedom of the press. Thomas Jefferson wrote after the war, "The first misfortune of the Revolutionary war induced a motion to suppress or garble the account of it. It was rejected with indignation."[19] Another, possibly more cynical explanation for the lack of action was Congress' fear of demonstrating its powerlessness.[20]

Censorship in the War of 1812

The lack of punishment of censorship violations during the Revolution was repeated during the War of 1812. There was little change in the delay in publishing war news, again removing any impetus to censor the publication of operational information.

Though the war did bring limited reporting on the field of battle, little censorship resulted. When the reporter who was probably the first American war correspondent, James M. Bradford of the *Time Piece* of St. Francisville, Louisiana, enlisted in Andrew Jackson's army

and filed dispatches during the Battle of New Orleans, no
effort to censor them is recorded.[21]

One case of censorship did occur shortly after the
Battle of New Orleans. *The Louisiana Gazette* wrote that
Jackson had received word of peace between the United
States and England.'[22] Jackson ordered the editor to seek
his permission before printing any more on the subject.[23]
In the ensuing uproar Jackson, using his authority under
martial law, imprisoned and court-martialed a Louisiana
state legislator who authored an article protesting the
order, and expelled from New Orleans a judge who had
ordered the legislator released. The incident ended when
Jackson was forced by a U.S. court to pay civil damages for
his actions.[24]

Censorship in the Mexican War

Several changes occurred in the reporting of the
Mexican War which could have brought widespread censorship.
The first change was the large number of correspondents
accompanying Zachary Taylor's and Winfield Scott's armies
into Mexico. Dozens of correspondents writing for sharply
competitive newspapers throughout the U.S. reported every
event of the war in detail.[25]

A second change, one familiar today to any watcher
of the *Cable News Network*, was that press reports of events
in the war appeared days or even weeks ahead of official
reports.[26] The efficiency of Mexican War reporting had its

11

root in the use of new technology (the telegraph, the railroad and the steamship) as well as the use of dispatch riders based both in Mexico and in the U.S. who quickly carried war news to editors.

Newspaper dispatch riders carried correspondents' dispatches across Mexico to Vera Cruz or Point Isabel, Mexican ports on the Gulf of Mexico. A steamer could then carry them to New Orleans in as little as three to five days.[27] New Orleans newspapers bearing war news were carried by dispatch riders to Washington, where the stories were telegraphed or carried by rail throughout the east. Even the text of the peace treaty ending the war reached Washington days before the actual treaty arrived. The government learned of the treaty through the press.[28]

These changes could have brought attempts by commanders in the field, especially Zachary Taylor and Winfield Scott, to censor all correspondents' dispatches to prevent them from providing information to aid the Mexicans. Though several newspapers were suppressed and correspondents endured "occasional uses of censorship and other forms of press harassment,"[29] no widespread censorship took place. Several factors prevented commanders from taking this action.

First, aside from the fact that few dispatches carried much information of any significance to the Mexicans, many of them did contain a "palpable intention to

flatter certain commanders," or were a "chronicle of
'thrilling achievements' by our 'gallant troops.'"[30] Since
the Mexican War was relatively short and successful and
there was no evidence that newspaper accounts aided the
Mexicans, there was no need to stifle criticism. On the
contrary, the flattery heaped on Zachary Taylor by these
correspondents almost certainly propelled him into the
presidency.

Second, the presence of the correspondents on the
campaign and the service they provided was not looked on as
being undesirable by the commanders. For the first time,
correspondents provided their newspapers with "detailed
lists of battle casualties."[31] The publishing of these
lists became the first reliable next-of-kin notification
system for casualties in an American war.

Most correspondents were combatants. Many served
as "honorary" aides-de-camp, providing valuable staff
assistance to the commanders. Several correspondents or
their assistants were killed or wounded in action while
serving as combatants.

In addition, the efficient courier systems created
by the correspondents to carry their dispatches were
allowed to operate without interference. On several
occasions, both Scott and Taylor used these systems to send
official dispatches when their own couriers were killed by
guerrillas.[32] U.S. commanders in the Mexican War did not

object to the presence of correspondents and had little to
gain through alienating them by enforcing widespread
censorship.

Censorship in the American Civil War

The decision to enforce censorship in the Civil War
could not be ignored by the leaders of Union and the
Confederacy. Large numbers of reporters wrote at length on
the war for audiences whose enthusiasm for the war wavered
but enthusiasm for war news did not. New York newspapers
often devoted one-third of their writing to the war.[33]
This clamor for war news and the speed with which war news
could be published--a legacy of the technological changes
in reporting introduced in the Mexican War, with the
addition of field photography--caused the leaders of both
sides to consider unprecedented control of the press.

Wartime Press Censorship in the North

In the North, during and after the Fort Sumter
crisis, the implementation of censorship proved haphazard.
The Northern press, for example, had access to and wrote
about the contents of official reports before the Federal
government received them. The report of Union Major Robert
Anderson announcing the surrender of his Fort Sumter
garrison was provided verbatim to the Northern press prior
to its being telegraphed to Washington. Thus the first
stories on the beginning of the conflict were printed
before the government received the report.[34]

The Northern government's first concern was with the protection of information on military operations. At the beginning of the war, Union commanding general Winfield Scott, worried about news of troop movements being provided to the enemy by reporters, 'complained in fact that he would prefer a hundred spies in any camp to one reporter.'[35]

The first attempts at censorship in the North were aimed at the Washington telegraph wire. While some use of the hundreds of miles of telegraph lines in the northeast U.S. had been used to report the Mexican War, the tens of thousands of miles of telegraph wire available to reporters in 1861 made their large-scale use possible.[36]

In April 1861, Secretary of State William H. Seward stopped the transmission of press reports on Union troop movements over Washington telegraph lines.[37] He finally formalized this practice with his July 1861 order appointing a censor to 'prune outgoing (Washington) telegrams of anything supposedly helpful to rebellion.'[38]

Censorship of telegraph lines followed the Union forces to the field. The commander of the Union forces in Washington, Irwin McDowell, informed reporters that 'no further dispatches relating to the army's movements . . . and no newspaper reports of any character would be transmitted' until reviewed by his staff.[39] Since all telegraphic communication with Union forces in the field was routed through Washington, censorship followed the army as it maneuvered in Virginia for the Battle of Bull Run in July 1861.

Immediately before the battle, however, General Scott reached an agreement with reporters permitting the uncensored use of the telegraph to report the "progress and results of all battles actually occurring" and other war news within certain guidelines.[40] The actual agreement is the first recorded use of ground rules. The agreement read in part:

> 1. That no reports of arrivals, departures or other movements of troops shall be forwarded by telegraph, nor any statistics of army numbers or munitions;
> 2. That no mutinies or riots among the soldiery be telegraphed;
> 3. Nor any predictions of movements to ensue.[41]

The agreement held for all of nine days. When General Scott learned of the rout of Union forces at Bull Run, he reimposed strict censorship on the telegraph.[42]

Censorship of telegraph reports remained haphazard and indiscriminate throughout the war. Reporters supportive of the government endured little or no censorship. The reports of *New York Tribune* reporter Samuel Wilkeson, a favorite of Secretary of War Simon Cameron, were "permitted to go out without censorship."[43]

Even opposition to the government was not necessarily cause for greater restriction. The respected

Washington reporter "Shad" Adams of the Democratic

opposition's *New York World* was in:

> . . . high standing among government officials.
> Even the telegraph censor, Benjamin P. Snyder,
> frequently permitted Adams to send out dispatches
> without submitting them for prior examination,
> simply on the strength of Adams' assurance that the
> material they contained was "all right."[44]

Even when censorship was strictly imposed, there

were few restrictions on what appeared in newspapers,

provided the reporter could get his copy to the printer

(and as long as the administration did not take affront to

the reporting and close the publication or arrest its

publisher). When General Scott reimposed censorship of the

telegraph lines after the disaster at Bull Run, reporters

merely left the battle on horseback or passenger trains to

file their stories.[45]

Other reporters went to greater lengths to

circumvent censorship. Before the Battle of Antietam, the

Washington correspondent for the *New York Herald* wrote in a

letter to his paper:

> You desire that everything in reference to the
> campaign in Maryland shall be sent by telegraph. I
> have tried in vain to comply with that request and
> find that all my dispatches, however carefully
> worded in regard to the position of affairs in
> Maryland are cut out, and, as the news is
> important, I have adopted the plan of sending
> everything of that kind by mail in order to secure
> its transmission.[46]

George W. Smalley of the *New York Tribune* avoided

censorship while reporting the same battle by riding:

. . . for six hours before he reached a telegraph
office. After he persuaded the operator to accept
his message, it was not sent to his paper, but to
Washington, where it was held up for six hours
before being forwarded to New York. Smalley could
not get a wire for his main story and had to carry
it to New York himself, writing it on the train.[47]

The State Department's control of the Washington
telegraph continued until Congress concluded a series of
hearings critical of the suppression of political
commentary by the State Department censor. In February
1862, Congress caused the telegraphic censorship
responsibility to be given to the War Department.[48]

A second technological change which could have
resulted in censorship was the capability to record and
publish images of the war by illustrators or photographers.
The first, the widespread use of detailed, lifelike
woodcuts in newspapers and weekly magazines, depicted not
only battlefield scenes and nearly photographic likenesses
of 'leading wartime figures' but also campaign maps
depicting troop dispositions and movements.[49] Hundreds of
artists published thousands of illustrations during the war
(*Harper's Weekly* and *Frank Leslie's Illustrated Weekly*
alone employed nearly 80 artists and published more than
3,000 illustrations),[50] but were infrequent targets of
censorship. One reaction to a censorship violation over
the publishing of illustrations was the banning by Major
General George B. McClellan of the *Harper's Weekly* from the

camps of the Army of the Potomac during the spring of 1862 for 'printing sketches of McClellan's siege works.'[51]

The other capability to record and publish images of the war, by photograph, was made possible by the celebrity status of photographer Matthew Brady. The ubiquitous Brady and his associates took more than 3,500 photographs of the conflict from Fort Sumter to Appomattox with the permission of President Lincoln and under the protection of the Secret Service.[52] Since no technology had been developed to allow printers to include photographs in their publications, any impetus to censor their publication was stilled.[53] Though the graphic nature of these photographs was at times disquieting, no recorded attempt to censor photographs survives.

A second attempt at voluntary censorship of war reporting occurred after the Bull Run failure of voluntary censorship. This agreement with reporters was made by the new commander of Union forces in Washington, McClellan. His arrival in the capitol was greeted by reporters with optimism. Within two days of his assuming command of the Army of the Potomac, he met with the press and:

> . . . promised to extend every possible facility for obtaining information to the newspapermen, but on two points would insist on complete secrecy; (1) no publication of the arrival of new regiments in Washington; (2) no mention of any movements or future plans of the army.[54]

McClellan quickly followed the meeting with a formal agreement with the Washington press corps. This

agreement, as General Scott's agreement had the month
before, permitted the uncensored use of the telegraph to
report war news within certain guidelines.[55] The agreement
read in part:

> 1st: That all such editors be requested to
> refrain from publishing, either as editorial or as
> correspondence, of any description or from any
> point any matter that may furnish aid and comfort
> to the enemy;
> 2d: That they may be also requested and
> earnestly solicited to signify their correspondents
> here and elsewhere their approval of the foregoing
> suggestion and to comply with it in spirit and
> letter;
> Also resolved: That the Government be
> respectfully requested to afford to the
> representatives of the Press facilities for
> obtaining and immediately transmitting all
> information suitable for publication, particularly
> touching engagements with the enemy.[56]

This agreement, like the first attempt at voluntary
censorship, was short-lived. Three days after it was
signed, articles appeared in the *New York Times* and the *New
York Tribune* concerning an ineptly-led Union campaign in
what is now West Virginia. The circumstances of how these
articles were researched, written, and reacted to by the
Northern leadership are representative of the problems of
censorship during the Civil War and quickly put an end to
voluntary censorship.

William Swinton of the *New York Times* and Albert D.
Richardson of the *New York Tribune* travelled in July 1861
to the western Virginia headquarters of Jacob D. Cox, the
local Union commanding general. After presenting
themselves and their credentials to Cox, they requested

20

permission to accompany the Union column during upcoming
operations and asked that they be permitted to live at the
headquarters while writing about the campaign. These
requests, representative of Union field command practices
for dealing with reporters throughout the war, were
rejected by Cox. After some debate, Cox allowed them to
accompany the column but demanded that they provide their
stories to his staff for review prior to publication.
Outraged by their frosty reception and the threat of
censorship, the reporters assented to the condition. In
actuality neither would ever:

> . . . submit any of their letters to his staff for
> censorship.
>   Denied the fellowship and confidence of Cox's
> officers, alternately disciplined and ignored,
> Richardson and Swinton followed the expedition as
> outcasts [and] . . . so the two New York
> journalists discovered the shabby truth about the
> . . campaign.[57]

Denied access to the commander and his staff,
Richardson and Swinton went to the only source available:
any member of the command willing to talk. In many cases,
their sources were disgusted with Cox, an opinion obviously
shared by both reporters. Their reports, probably
retaliation for the contempt which the reporters felt they
had endured, were forwarded by mail to circumvent Cox's
censorship. The reports clearly portrayed Cox and his
command as ineffective and inept.[58]

Reaction by the Northern leadership was swift.
Their concerns were twofold. "Were newspapermen qualified

to pass judgement on general officers? Should
correspondents be permitted to destroy military careers by
harsh criticism?'[se] Their answer to these questions was
soon published in General Order 67, which declared that:

> . . . all correspondence and communication
> verbally, or by writing, printing or telegraphing'
> respecting operations of the army and affairs of
> the military or naval establishments were
> forbidden, except on authorization and with the
> consent of the commanding officer.[eo]

The attitudes of the Northern leadership had
hardened as a result of Richardson's and Swinson's critical
reporting. Since violation of General Order 67 also
violated the Articles of War, a reporter could face
execution for circumventing it. Censorship could no longer
be ignored.[ei]

The imposition of strict censorship followed
McClellan's army to the field for the Peninsula campaign in
the spring and summer of 1862. The delays inherent in
having a commander approve each outgoing reporter's
dispatch caused a considerable uproar. The dissatisfaction
with this system resulted in Secretary of War Edwin M.
Stanton's order for a 'parole system, which, in effect,
made each correspondent his own censor.'[ea] The order
contained some limitations. Each correspondent had to take
a loyalty oath to the U.S. and had to swear that:

> He would not write, make or transmit any
> intelligence, opinion, statement, drawing, or plan
> that would give or tend to give aid or comfort to
> the enemy. He further was required to avoid making

any reference in his correspondence to the following:

1. The location or change of location of headquarters of generals, as well as the names of generals, regiments, brigades, or divisions in the field "except when engagements have taken place."

2. The number of regiments, brigades, divisions, batteries or pieces of artillery, or the proportion of cavalry in service at any point.

3. The kind of arms or ammunition used or the number of days' rations served.

4. The number of transports used for any movement, the description of any movement, until after its objective had been accomplished or defeated, allusions to the object of movements or suggestions of future movements or attacks.

5. The position or location of camps, pickets, or outposts.

6. Pictorial representations of Federal fortifications or lines of defenses.[63]

These restrictions were not enforced and were therefore ignored by the correspondents. One explanation for the lack of enforcement was that the restrictions were carried in a voluminous document, too long to be read by guards. Any reporter presenting the voluminous "parole" would be passed by a guard who did not want to "take the trouble of reading through it."[64]

In the West, Major General Henry Halleck became exasperated with what he perceived to be unwarranted criticism and meddling in his campaign by reporters. He issued an order which "demanded the removal of 'unauthorized persons' from the camps" to an area "nearly twenty miles to the rear."[65] The order resulted in the expulsion of all reporters from the area of operations of the army and stirred controversy which lasted throughout the war.

Arguments Used in the North Against Censorship

The basic problem which boiled to the surface in the ensuing uproar was the conflicting requirements of traditional press freedom and the requirements of a government managing a war. The banning of reporters by Halleck launched a series of attacks in the press against "the scissoring of military intelligence tidbits from press dispatches."** These attacks typified five arguments used by the press against censorship during the Civil War.

The first argument by the press against censorship during the Civil War was that censorship was unnecessary because it was not completely effective. "Any rebel spy . . . may count each regiment, battalion and squadron in Missouri . . . enforced secrecy was thus 'the merest pantomime.'" In addition, reporters argued that senior Union officers "let their tongues wag freely" letting slip more information than any newspaper ever could.**

Another reason censorship was cited as being ineffective was that one mistake by a censor ruined any possible censorship benefit. A censor was "like a high wire artist. One slip and he was off the program."**

The second argument by the press against censorship was that the way censorship was implemented was inconsistent and exhibited favoritism. It was argued that news cut from dispatches to one paper were allowed to pass in dispatches to other papers. Contradictory censorship

orders from field commanders and the Secretary of War were
repeatedly the targets of editorial criticism.[69] Charges
and countercharges of favoritism were rampant:

> The *New York Tribune* charged that General Grant
> gave reports on the battle of Shiloh, which were
> withheld from other correspondents, to a pet
> reporter of the *New York Herald*; the *Herald* accused
> the *Tribune* of printing secret information from
> McClellan's army in order to hasten the downfall of
> the young commander and his replacement with a
> general more hospitable to Greeley's
> abolitionism.[70]

The third complaint by the press against censorship
was that it did not apply to soldiers and civilians other
than reporters. The argument went that 'generals,
privates, chaplains, doctors and contractors' wrote letters
to the press 'bubbling enthusiastically with any military
plan they knew' whether the plans were true or not. Since
many 'irresponsible' papers printed these letters, the
'experienced' press argued that 'the only way to defeat
error was by giving a free rein to truth.'[71]

The fourth argument against censorship was that it
was merely a shield for the vanity of senior Union
officers.

> Truthful reporting, said some correspondents,
> irked only 'ex-butcher boys, country pedagogues,
> and counter-jumpers, elevated into positions of
> small trust.' Also . . . no complaint was ever
> made about correspondents who flattered commanders.
> It was the general who was all 'sword, plume and
> buttons,' the thieving supply officer, the military
> men used only to the reports of 'parasites and
> toadies' who found the fierce white light of
> criticism unbearable.[72]

The final argument voiced during the war was that censorship violated America's traditional freedom of the press. 'When a government is loudly calling for more men and money,' wrote one correspondent, 'should it not at least be willing to entrust that people with a knowledge of what is going on?' The 'right of the people to know' slammed headlong into the government's ownership of 'what was more important, the last word.'[73]

Throughout the remainder of the war, the government's handling of major actions remained similar. As a major battle or campaign occurred, little information passed the censor. As the results of a battle or campaign trickled north, the government allowed additional information to pass the censor, though often changing casualty figures or other details to soften the news of defeats.[74]

Correspondents were particularly annoyed by Secretary of War Stanton's habit of censoring 'truthful accounts of (Union) reverses and losses.'[75] When *New York Herald* reporter Sylvanus Cadwallader complained that he would not 'submit to such interference except on compulsion, the Army officer assigned as the Washington telegraphic censor replied:

> 'What do you plan to do about it?' To this I vouchsafed no reply.
> Within an hour I engaged three intelligent men . . . to act as messengers in carrying *New York Herald* dispatches . . . all correspondence could be delivered at the *Herald* office . . . free from

military censorship by mail or telegraph; and
appear in the same issue of the *Herald* as if
telegraphed from Washington.[76]

By far the most controversial and far reaching
problem of censorship during the Civil War was the
discretion authorized commanding generals in the field in
their dealings with reporters. The uproar caused by
Halleck's ban on reporters has been discussed earlier. The
conduct of censorship by Union commanders in the field,
when backed by the threat of execution posed by the
Articles of War, remains controversial even today.

In February 1862, several district commanders in
the West ordered the suppression of the circulation of the
Chicago Times for printing material they objected to.
Enforcement of the order included the arrest of vendors and
the confiscation and destruction of any papers they
carried. When the commander in the West, Ulysses Grant,
learned of the ban:

> . . . while he objected to the general tenor of the
> *Times* as much as any officer in his Dep't. he
> nevertheless admitted the right of anyone to pay
> for it and read it. A special order was sent to
> those officers countermanding their action.[77]

Brigadier General Benjamin F. Butler, quoted in
1861 as suggesting that 'the Government would not
accomplish much until it had hanged . . . half a dozen
spies and at least one reporter,'[78] issued an order in 1861
similar to Halleck's ban on reporters. Butler 'decreed the
expulsion from his department of any person who gave

information of movements of troops."[78] Unlike Halleck's order, Butler's was not enforced.

While other Union generals ranted at the press and arrested or otherwise intimidated reporters throughout the war, the activity of one commander stands out. William T. Sherman spoke of reporters as "infamous dogs," "buzzards," "paid spies," and "little whippersnappers . . . too lazy, idle and cowardly to be soldiers."[80]

Sherman's censorship technique was simple. "When a reporter approached him for information as to his forces, he ordered the man to leave camp in fifteen minutes or be hanged as a spy."[81] He told another reporter that "the next train for Louisville goes at half-past one. Take that train!"[82]

When the *New York Herald*'s Thomas W. Knox wrote a news report critical of Sherman's handling of the Vicksburg campaign, Sherman had him arrested and court-martialed. Though charged with violating the Articles of War, he was acquitted:[83]

> Even to please the commanding general, the court-martial could hardly have hanged him for conveying information to the enemy in a letter printed nearly three weeks after the engagement. He was . . . sent out of the zone of operations.[84]

Sherman ordered the arrest of Randolph Keim of the *New York Herald* after he wrote a "minute account of the Confederate Signal Code just then discovered by Federal Commanders." Only a warning from sympathetic Army officers which allowed his escape from the area saved Keim from court martial.[85]

When embarking on his campaign which ended in the 'March to the Sea,' Sherman ordered 'that if any newspaperman was found accompanying the army he was to be tried by a drumhead court-martial and shot before breakfast.'[86] The threat was not all hot air.

When the *Chicago Journal* printed a report from their correspondent who had managed to accompany the army, Sherman ordered 'his immediate arrest as a spy and trial by court-martial.' The reporter 'decamped the army in great haste.'[87]

A particularly effective method of enforcing censorship of the press in the North was through the suspension of the writ of habeas corpus, and the imprisonment and or trial of publishers critical of the administration. In addition, several newspapers were closed by the government while their publishers were in jail.[88]

Wartime Press Censorship in the South

Censorship in the north during the Civil War was haphazard, arbitrary, and inconsistent. In contrast to northern ineffectiveness, Confederate wartime press censorship is generally considered to have been more effective.[89] There were three significant differences in southern and northern press censorship.

The first difference was that the "letter correspondence of Southern newspapermen was censored at the source only on rare occasions."[90] This contrasts sharply with the routine censorship of the correspondence of northern newspapermen.

A second difference was the existence throughout the war of successful voluntary censorship guidelines.

> Forbidden news topics were the movements of Confederate troops, munitions of war, gunboats, or batteries, and the descriptions and locations of forts. It was permissible, on the other hand, to publish all movements of the enemy fortifications and munitions of war, "and all intelligence of our own movements taken from northern papers, without giving additional authenticity to the same."[91]

To voluntary censorship, however, censorship regulations were added. Telegraphic censorship similar to that in the north was imposed,[92] and a series of censorship orders were published. One order, issued in 1862, placed "restrictions on the reporting of the positions of Confederate troops."[93] Another order, issued in 1864, threatened to court-martial officers or soldiers authoring "any article regarding troop movements for publication less than one month after the campaign had ended."[94]

The final difference between northern and southern press censorship was that the freedom enjoyed by northern commanding generals in the field in dealing with reporters was not shared by their Confederate counterparts. While Confederate generals did restrict reporters from accompanying their forces and at times required reporters'

30

dispatches to be submitted for their review,[85] other
restrictive measures common in the north were not allowed.
When a Confederate general issued an order in 1862
threatening to fine and imprison editors critical of
military officers in his command, the Confederate Congress
passed a resolution to limit such abuses of power.[86]

     In general, Confederate authorities used their
reticence to comment on their army's activities as a method
of restricting the publication of security information by
southern newspapers. In contrast to loose-lipped Union
senior officers, when a reporter asked a southern staff
officer for war news he would typically receive the pompous
reply:

     . . . 'We have nothing;' when, at the same time,
     the enquirer for war news has private dispatches in
     his pocket that fighting has been going on all day
     at the point specified.[87]

     Activities that were looked on as restrictive and
as censorship in the north were accepted as normal
operations in the south. When reporters were excluded from
campaigns, or restricted from or expelled from camps,
little objection was raised.[88] The repeated successes of
Confederate forces and the comparatively united population
of the Confederacy combined to make these restrictions more
palatable. Not until repeated defeats faced the
Confederacy did the southern press become critical of
censorship restrictions.[89]

Conclusions

The English colonists brought government control of the press and harsh punishment for offensive writing to America. Despite this heritage, there were few attempts to censor war news during the Revolutionary War or the War of 1812. Changes in the Mexican War which increased the level of censorship were the dozens of correspondents reporting from the field of battle and their efficient use of the telegraph, railroads, steamships, and dispatch riders to quickly carry war news to editors.

The numbers of correspondents and their speedy reporting using these technological improvements were repeated in the Civil War. These factors caused leaders of both sides to implement widespread control of the press. The issue which faced the belligerents was the conflicting requirements of traditional U.S. press freedom versus the requirements of a government managing a war. In contrast to northern ineffectiveness, Confederate wartime press censorship was more effective. While the north chafed under censorship restrictions, the Confederacy accepted them with little objection until Confederate forces suffered repeated defeats.

CHAPTER 2 ENDNOTES

1. Harold L. Nelson, and John L. Teeter, Jr., *Law of Mass Communications*, 6th ed., (New York: Foundation Press, 1989), p. 54.

2. James R. Wiggins, *Freedom or Secrecy* (New York: Oxford University Press, 1964), p. 94.

3. Nelson and Teeter, p. 23.

4. Ibid., p. 24.

5. Frederic Hudson, *Journalism in the United States From 1690 to 1872* (New York: Harper & Brothers, 1873), p. 48.

6. Ibid.

7. John B. McMaster, *Benjamin Franklin as a Man of Letters* (Boston: Houghton, Mifflin and Co., 1900), pp. 26-27.

8. Carl Van Doren, *Benjamin Franklin* (New York: Viking Press, 1938), p. 27.

9. Frank L. Mott, *American Journalism, A History: 1690-1960* (Toronto: MacMillan and Company, 1969), pp. 19-20.

10. Hudson, p. 52.

11. Ibid.

12. James R. Wiggins, *Freedom or Secrecy* (New York: Oxford University Press, 1964), p. 94.

13. Bernard Bailyn and John B. Hench, eds., *The Press and the American Revolution* (Worcester: American Antiquarian Society, 1980), p. 80.

14. Ibid., p. 81.

15. David M. O'Brien, *The Public's Right to Know: The Supreme Court and the First Amendment* (New York: Praeger, 1981), p. 36.

16. Mott, p. 99.

17. Ibid., pp. 100-101.

18. William Greider, "The Press as Adversary," *Washington Post*, 27 June 1971, p. B1.

19. Wiggins, p. 94.

20. Bailyn and Hench, pp. 81-82.

21. Mott, p. 196.

22. James R. Mock, *Censorship 1917* (Princeton, NJ: Princeton University Press, 1941), p. 9.

23. Ibid.

24. Robert V. Remini, *The Life of Andrew Jackson* (New York: Harper and Row, 1988), p. 109.

25. Mott, p. 249.

26. F. Lauriston Bullard, *Famous War Correspondents* (Boston: Little, Brown and Co., 1914), pp. 364-65.

27. Bullard, pp. 370-372.

28. Ibid., p. 373.

29. Edwin and Michael Emery, *The Press and America: An Interpretative History*, 4th ed., (Englewood Cliffs: Prentice Hall, 1978), p. 144.

30. Bullard, p. 353.

31. Edwin & Michael Emery, *The Press and America: An Interpretative History*, 5th ed. (Englewood Cliffs, Prentice Hall, 1984), p. 166.

32. Bullard, pp. 371-72.

33. Emery, 5th ed., pp. 195-96.

34. Emmet Crozier, *Yankee Reporters* (New York: Oxford University Press, 1956), pp. 51-53.

35. Bernard A. Weisberger, *Reporters for the Union* (Boston: Little, Brown and Company, 1953), p. 79.

36. Phillip Knightley, *The First Casualty* (New York: Harcourt, Brace, Jovanovich, 1976), p. 20.

37. J. Cutler Andrews, *The North Reports the Civil War* (Pittsburgh: University of Pittsburgh Press, 1955), p. 94.

38. Ibid., p. 85.

39. Crozier, p. 86.

40. Andrews, *The North Reports the Civil War*, p. 94.

41. Crozier, p. 88.

42. Andrews, *The North Reports the Civil War*, p. 95.

43. Ibid., p. 56.

44. Ibid., p. 46.

45. Ibid., p. 93.

46. Ibid., p. 271.

47. Mott, p. 335.

48. Weisberger, p. 91; and Andrews, *The North Reports the Civil War*, p. 95.

49. Emery, 5th ed., p. 203.

50. Knightley, p. 20.

51. Weisberger, p. 95.

52. Emery, 5th ed., p. 205.

53. Knightley, p. 20; and Jorge Lewinski, *The Camera at War*, (New York: Simon and Schuster, 1978) pp. 44-46.

54. Crozier, p. 133.

55. Ibid., p. 134.

56. Harold L. Nelson, ed., *Freedom of the Press from Hamilton to the Warren Court* (Indianapolis: Bobbs-Merrill, 1967), p. 208.

57. Crozier, p. 141.

58. Ibid., pp. 142-43.

59. Ibid.

60. Ibid., p. 135.

61. Ibid.; and Andrews, *The North Reports the Civil War*, p. 151.

62. Andrews, *The North Reports the Civil War*, p. 196.

63. Ibid.

64. Ibid.

65. Weisberger, p. 97.

66. Ibid., p. 98.

67. Ibid.

68. Ibid.

69. Ibid., pp. 100-101.

70. Ibid.

71. Ibid., pp. 101-2.

72. Ibid., p. 103.

73. Ibid., p. 104.

74. Andrews, *The North Reports the Civil War*, pp. 649-650; and Knightley, p. 27.

75. Sylvanus Cadwallader, *Three Years With Grant*, (New York: Alfred A. Knopf, 1956), p. 219.

76. Ibid.

77. Ibid., pp. 56-57.

78. Weisberger, p. 79.

79. Ibid.

80. Andrews, *The North Reports the Civil War*, p. 115.

81. Weisberger, p. 93.

82. Andrews, *The North Reports the Civil War*, p. 115.

83. Cadwallader, p. 45.

84. Ibid., pp. 113-14.

85. Cadwallader, pp. 97-98.

86. Andrews, *The North Reports the Civil War*, p. 552.

87. Ibid., p. 553.

88. Mock, pp. 10-11.

89. J. Cutler Andrews, *The South Reports the Civil War* (Princeton: Princeton University Press, 1970), p. 533.

90. Ibid., p. 529.

91. Ibid., p. 530.

92. Ibid., pp. 61, 343.

93. Ibid., p. 532.

94. Ibid., p. 533.

95. Ibid., p. 173.

96. Ibid., p. 532.

97. Ibid., p. 531.

98. Ibid., pp. 81, 103.

99. Ibid., pp. 149-50.

CHAPTER 3

U.S. WARTIME PRESS CENSORSHIP FROM THE
SPANISH-AMERICAN WAR THROUGH WORLD WAR I

On the night of 15 February 1898, the U.S. battleship *Maine* exploded and sank in Havana Harbor. Dozens of American reporters in Cuba covering the rebellion against Spain duly reported the incident and sent America and Spain spiraling toward war.[1]

The report to Washington of the explosion by the captain of the *Maine* was carried by New York *Herald* reporter George Bronson Rea to the only telegraph cable in Cuba connecting with the U.S., a Spanish operated cable in Havana. This report was allowed to be transmitted by the Spanish censor, as were a short report from the Associated Press and a report sent by New York *World* reporter Sylvester Scovel on 'a stolen cable blank containing the censor's stamp of approval.'[2] No other dispatches about the destruction of the Maine passed the Spanish censors.[3]

This legacy of tight censorship by the Spanish in Cuba together with the fierce competition for news in the U.S. set the stage for the implementation of censorship by the U.S. upon the declaration of war in April 1898.

The first battle of the Spanish-American War did not see censorship invoked. Three reporters accompanied Admiral Dewey's U.S. Asiatic Squadron from Hong Kong for its attack on the Spanish fleet in Manila. Dewey asked the reporters to report "nothing which would disclose the fleet movements to Spain, since the information could be relayed to Manila."[4]

One reporter violated this request, and surreptitiously dispatched stories to the New York *World* stating that "Philippine insurgents were ready to invest the approaches to Manila" and that Dewey's squadron would depart for the Philippines on April 26th and attack Manila on April 30th.[5] The squadron actually departed for the Philippines on the 26th and attacked Manila at dawn on May 1st.[6] Despite the access of the Spanish to these New York *World* stories, the U.S. squadron destroyed the Spanish fleet. This potential for publication of operational information would not be ignored in other U.S. operations during the war.

In the Caribbean, severe Spanish censorship of the Havana to Key West, Florida, telegraph line persisted after the destruction of the *Maine*. The press resorted to the hiring of small "dispatch" boats. These were used to circumvent the censorship by transporting reports directly to the Key West telegraph office and remained in use throughout the war.[7]

Following the declaration of war, the U.S.
Department of War planned operations against Spanish troops
in Cuba and Puerto Rico. Shortly after the destruction of
the *Maine*, the U.S. began a naval blockade of Cuba.[9] Prior
to the departure for Cuba of the U.S. blockade fleet, in
Key West, Tampa and New York the Navy Department or the
U.S. Army "Signal Corps put a censor in each of the
cable company offices."[9] Initially the censorship was not
strict:

> Cipher [encoded] messages were forbidden to the
> West Indies [and Spain or her possessions] [as
> were] any messages in plain text which conveyed
> important information concerning military
> operations or such as were detrimental to the
> interests of the country.[10]

Such liberal censorship was short-lived. A small
steamer, the *Gussie*, was ordered to take supplies from
Tampa to the Cuban coast near Havana for Cuban insurgents
friendly to the U.S. The censorship policy was abused
when:

> Despite vows of secrecy that correspondents
> were sworn to, the expedition was about as well
> advertised as the arrival of a circus in town. The
> Atlanta *Constitution* headlined the story: "Cuban
> Invasion Commences Today." The New York *Tribune's*
> story mentioned the so-called "secrecy" in
> announcing the sailing: "The utmost secrecy is
> maintained regarding the point of landing, but in
> view of [a previous] landing near Havana . . . it
> is believed the expedition will be headed for a
> point not far from Havana."[11]

The liberal censorship policy allowed U.S.
newspaper stories (and press dispatch boats) to follow the
progress of the hapless steamer and her U.S. Navy escorts

to Cuba. Understandably, Spanish troops met the *Gussie* at
her landing point, and eventually sent her back to the U.S.
without landing her supplies. Since war news was slow,
U.S. newspapers devoted considerable space to vicious
criticism of every detail of the abortive operation. This
criticism combined with the abuse of the censorship policy
to bring a backlash of harsh censorship.[12] The U.S. Army
issued the following notice:

> The United States authorities declare that all
> messages containing information of prospective
> naval movements and current military operations are
> inimical to the United States, and are consequently
> forbidden. Senders of press or other messages are
> requested not to include such matter. If any such
> is found it will be stricken out by the censor.[13]

The new policy was immediately felt. Reporters
found the censorship 'absolute in connection with the
movements of all armed expeditions and vessels of war.'[14]

During May 1898, at the request of the U.S. Army,
Western Union allowed their Florida cable offices in Miami
and Jacksonville to be censored.[15] This censorship
remained in effect for the remainder of the war and limited
press reports to only those cleared by the censors:

> This meant that any confidential information
> correspondents might learn . . . could only reach
> the newspaper by dispatch boat or mail. By the
> time the boat or letter could get to New York, or
> to other places outside Florida, the news was
> stale.[16]

The effectiveness of the new censorship
restrictions was felt in the successful mission of a second
supply steamer to Cuba one week after the *Gussie* failure.

The efforts to prevent the publication of information about

this mission extended past cable restrictions:

> Each correspondent was notified that he would
> be held responsible if anything concerning the
> expedition appeared in the newspaper he represented
> . . . He was also notified to inform his paper that
> his credentials would be revoked in case the above
> instructions were violated.[17]

In addition to threats to prevent reporters from

accompanying U.S. forces to Cuba, the Army took other steps

besides censorship to prevent information "regarding the

projected movements of bodies of troops, naval vessels, and

transports from reaching the press."[18] Prior to the U.S.

invasion of Cuba, a New York *Journal* dispatch boat was

boarded in Tampa by U.S. soldiers and prevented from

sailing because reporters on the vessel were "suspected of

having obtained government plans and documents and intended

to sail for some port where they could send the matter by

wire."[19]

The censorship was conducted for the most part by

civilian telegraph employees. Censorship responsibility

fell on:

> At least two sworn assistants in each of the
> cable companies' transmitting offices who were
> citizens of the United States, and who made oath to
> faithfully observe the orders of the military
> censor.[20]

Despite its effectiveness, the imposition of the

censorship restrictions was haphazard, and was often

objectionable to reporters. The chief complaint

correspondents had with the censorship was often simply who conducted it:

> The first responsibility [was] on the correspondents and after them the Western Union Telegraph Company. Every telegraph operator was his own censor, and when he did not like the stuff in copy, he just cut it out to suit himself. Jacksonville took another rap at the copy, and by the time it reached the home office it was liable to be anything the writer did not intend.[21]

Another measure of the effectiveness of the censorship restrictions was the absence from U.S. newspapers of accurate information on the U.S. invasion of Cuba. The restrictive censorship was so effective and competition for news so fierce that many major New York newspapers began fabricating stories on the invasion:

> The New York *Journal*, never guilty of letting the truth stand in the way of a good story, dispensed with speculation and launched upon a series of fabrications almost without parallel in newspaper history. They proved such a boost to circulation that other New York papers soon fell into line and began copying the *Journal's* exclusives.[22]

Another method newspapers used in their attempts to circumvent the new restrictions was the use of encoded dispatches. These efforts proved fruitless since the censors stopped the transmission of any material that appeared to be in code and 'everything that was not absolutely plain and explainable.'[23]

The restrictive censorship in the Caribbean continued after the June 1898 landings in Cuba and the U.S. Army took control of all telegraph and telephone

43

communications on the island.[24] The censorship for the
month-long campaign in Cuba was a subject for editorial
humor in many U.S. newspapers. The Atlanta *Constitution*
printed a poem entitled 'The Censor:'

> Have they met?
>   Have they fought?
> Has the Spaniard
>   Been caught?
> Have they shelled him
> And felled him
> And buried and knelled him?
> The sphinx of a censor
>   Says naught!
>
> Have they met?
>   Have they fought?
> Has the havoc
>   Been wrought?
> Have they tripped him
> And nipped him
> And collard [sic] and clipped him?
> The sphinx of censor
>   Says naught![25]

The tone of newspaper criticism of the censorship
and of U.S. Caribbean operations changed after the Spanish
capitulation in July 1898. The new criticism was based on
actions taken by the military command against reporters and
on restrictions on the reporting of the appalling living
conditions of the U.S. Army in Cuba.

Shortly after the Spanish capitulation, the U.S.
commander, Brigadier General Shafter, expelled all New York
Journal reporters from Cuba for inciting violence against
Spanish prisoners.[26] Despite requests from the War
Department, Shafter refused to allow the reporters to

return and said they 'deserved death. The *Journal* can send other men here if it chooses.'[27]

The second source of increased criticism was the censorship of reports on the number of soldiers killed or incapacitated by disease. No stories on the health of the army in Cuba were allowed to pass the censors. To circumvent the censorship restrictions, the stories were taken by dispatch boats to telegraph offices in Haiti and Jamaica to be cabled to the U.S. or were written by reporters who had returned to the U.S.[28]

Censorship in the Philippines

In the Philippines, Admiral Dewey's policy of limited censorship continued after the destruction of the Spanish fleet and the August 1898 occupation of Manila. In contrast to the vicious criticism heaped on U.S. operations in the Caribbean, Dewey received little criticism for either his censorship policies or his conduct of the Philippine operation.[29]

Dewey avoided criticism for several reasons, the first being his overwhelming victory in Manila. Another reason was he catered to the requirements of the handful of reporters who accompanied his squadron to the Philippines. He allowed reporters to use ships' boats for transportation and to operate from his ships during the battle. His famous words spoken on the bridge of the U.S. battleship *Olympia* at the beginning of the Battle of Manila Bay, 'You

45

may fire when ready, Gridley," were heard by a reporter standing at his side.[30]

The most significant reason for the lack of newspaper criticism of Dewey was his censorship policy. His policy was as lenient as the censorship policy in the Caribbean was extreme. Dewey told reporters:

> You are left largely to your own good and experienced judgement, not only as correspondents but as American citizens, but you will always bear in mind that you must not send what will give actual aid and comfort to the enemy, or that which will unduly excite and disturb the people at home.[31]

Dewey on several occasions at the request of correspondents "permitted information to be cabled" that his own censors had refused to transmit.[32]

The peace treaty between Spain and the U.S. was signed in December 1898. Accompanying the treaty was an insurrection by Filipino rebels led by Emilio Aguinaldo. Measures taken to combat the insurrection included a change in Dewey's lenient censorship policies.

The commander of operations to crush the rebels, U.S. Army Major General Ewell Otis, instituted strict censorship policies. These policies effectively prevented reports of "American suffering and American brutality" including the infamous "water cure torture" from appearing in U.S. newspapers until reporters left the Philippines and returned to the U.S. to file their stories.[33]

These stories also accused Otis of releasing
information which misrepresented the operations in the
Philippines. The reporters mailed reports to Hong Kong
which disclosed American failures and were critical of
Otis. Otis asked that the War Department prevent the ˙use
of the Hong Kong (telegraph) terminal by correspondents
. . . as it was the source of all the ˙detrimental reports
alarming the country.˙˙[34]

The continuing censorship restrictions exasperated
reporters. ˙My instructions,˙ one censor explained, ˙are
to shut off everything that could hurt the McKinley
administration.˙[35] Otis told reporters he had to ˙shield
the people from distortions and sensationalism.˙[36] The
newsmen, however, felt he used ˙censorship to conceal his
own failures.˙[37]

A representative group of reporters met with Otis
and told him that they had avoided reporting ˙sensations
that they had personally witnessed, such as American
soldiers bayoneting wounded *amigos* (Filipinos), the looting
of homes and churches, and so on.˙[38] The reporters agreed
to accept the censorship restrictions when Otis assured
them the war was nearly over and he expected the censorship
would soon be no longer necessary.[39] By July 1899,
however, the reporters were fed up.

The correspondents in Manila became so desperate
that they resorted to mailing to Hong Kong a cable to their

newspapers outlining their protests against Otis'

censorship policies:

> The undersigned, being all staff correspondents
> of American newspapers stationed in Manila, unite
> in the following statement:
> We believe that, owing to official despatches
> [sic] from Manila made public in Washington, the
> people of the United States have not received a
> correct impression of the situation in the
> Philippines, but that these despatches have
> presented an ultra-optimistic view that is not
> shared by the general officers in the field.
> We believe the despatches incorrectly represent
> the existing conditions among the Filipinos in
> respect to internal dissension and demoralization
> resulting from the American campaign and to the
> brigand character of their army.
> We believe the despatches err in the
> declaration that 'the situation is well in hand,'
> and in the assumption that the insurrection can be
> speedily ended without a greatly increased force.
> We think the tenacity of the Filipino purpose
> has been under-estimated, and that the statements
> are unfounded that volunteers are willing to engage
> in further service.
> The censorship has compelled us to participate
> in this misrepresentation by excising or altering
> uncontroverted statements of fact on the plea that
> 'they would alarm the people at home,' or 'have the
> people of the United State by their ears.'[40]

The controversy became so heated that the War

Department requested that Otis quietly remove the

censorship:

> Only continuing the requirement that all matter
> be submitted in advance, that you may deal, as you
> may deem best with any liable to affect military
> operations or offending against military
> discipline.[41]

Otis continued his policies and used another method

for censoring stories he felt 'gave the United States a

'black eye.'"[42] Many reporters were deported from the

Philippines for criticism:

Reporters who dared ask embarrassing questions were quickly deported and even President McKinley's personal representative was declared persona non grata for . . . [an] abusive article published in the San Francisco *Chronicle*.[43]

Otis repeatedly quieted criticism when he periodically announced that censorship had been abolished. Following these announcements, he simply appointed a new censor and continued rigid censorship "under the guise of correcting factual errors."[44] The Boston *Herald* found itself "in the awkward position of having congratulated Otis twice within the space of two months for having ended the censorship of news."[45]

The censorship policies became "increasingly arbitrary" as criticism mounted:

The word 'ambush' was scrubbed from dispatches, and correspondents could not mention defective ammunition after one reporter wrote that up to half the howitzer shells failed to explode on impact.[46]

Despite Otis's attempts to diffuse the criticism, the damage was done. Secretary of War Alger was forced to resign by the uproar over Otis's censorship policies and his own mishandling of the war.[47] Otis was shortly thereafter replaced by a Republican administration concerned he would be "a fearful stumbling block" in the November 1900 Presidential election.[48]

Telegraphic censorship continued under the new commander, Major General Arthur MacArthur, who assumed command in May 1900.[49] For the first time, incoming telegrams were also censored.[50] Censorship was eased in

December 1900. From that date reports could be telegraphed
to the U.S. without being censored as long as a copy of the
report was telegraphed to the military censor. Cables to
several other Philippine islands, however, were censored
throughout the remainder of the conflict.[81] This did not
prevent MacArthur from expelling one reporter who charged a
U.S. official with corruption as 'a dangerous incendiary
and menace to the military situation.'[82]

Censorship During the Mexican Interventions

During the short-lived U.S. military occupation of
Vera Cruz, Mexico, in 1914, telegraphic censorship was
again invoked. The censorship only extended to Vera Cruz
where it remained throughout the occupation. Efforts to
establish censorship at Galveston, Texas, were
unsuccessful.[83]

The censorship at Vera Cruz was haphazard. When a
New York *World* reporter attempted to file a story critical
of a British admiral, it was stopped by the censor. The
reporter informed the U.S. commander that he would mail the
story to the U.S., which he did without interference.[84]

Censorship during Pershing's Punitive Expedition
into Mexico in 1916 was equally fruitless. Though a censor
was appointed to 'whom all dispatches sent out by
correspondents were to be filed,'[85] the Army's inability to
restrict all forms of communication within the U.S. did not
permit effective censorship. For example, an Army censor

asked the editor of the Chicago *Herald*, James Keeley, to refrain from printing a story:

> That General Pershing had arrived at Columbus, New Mexico. Keeley did so, only to be informed from New York the next morning that some papers in that city carried the very information the *Herald* had suppressed [85]

One footnote to censorship during Pershing's Punitive Expedition was that the officer named as chief U.S. Army "military censor," in addition to his public relations duties, was then Major Douglas MacArthur. MacArthur earned accolades from the Washington press corps for his "patience and wise counsel" during the Mexican operation.[87]

Censorship in World War I

The U.S. declaration of war against Germany on April 6, 1917, did not herald the imposition of censorship restrictions. Restrictions had been in place for nearly a month. At the request of Secretary of War Daniels and during a conference of newspaper and State, War, and Navy Department representatives, newsmen were asked to submit to censorship restrictions "voluntarily, pending enactment of a press censorship law."[88] Despite several attempts immediately before and during the war, no censorship law passed.[89]

One element of the voluntary press censorship restrictions was the avoidance of publishing "shipping news."[90] Another element requested that:

> No information, reports, or rumors, attributing
> a policy to the government in any international
> situation, not authorized by the President or a
> member of the cabinet, be published without first
> consulting the Department of State.[81]

Similar regulations were added by the War and Navy

Departments.[82]

Shortly after the declaration of war, President

Woodrow Wilson created the Committee on Public Information.

The committee's primary role in the war was to create

positive publicity to convince the American people to

support the war. But the committee also:

> Supervised a voluntary censorship of the press
> [in the U.S.], which left the matter of news
> suppression up to the newspapers themselves . . .
> Approximately 99 percent of the press observed the
> rules of this voluntary censorship.[83]

The committee chief, George Creel, was used as "a

whipping-boy" after the war after a "realization of how war

hysteria had been utilized through propaganda

techniques."[84] This criticism and his committee's

"propaganda techniques" are outside the scope of this

discussion. However, his committee's domestic censorship

efforts are important in the overall view of World War I

press censorship.

Shortly after the committee's creation, it issued a

set of voluntary censorship restrictions for newspaper and

magazine publishers. These restrictions prohibited the

publishing of troop movements, ship sailings, and "other

events of strictly military character."[85] A longer, more

formal set of restrictions was issued in December 1917, and remained in force for the remainder of the war. It appears in full in Appendix 1.

This plan of voluntarily press censorship for the continental U.S. was later referred to by Creel as "a patriotic pledge with one hand on the heart and the other on the flag."[85] The effectiveness of the program, though it continued throughout the war, was poor. Creel wrote about the problems of administering voluntary censorship over the entire U.S.:

> Administration . . . had to be broken down to every metropolitan center, for it was obviously absurd to assume that San Francisco, Dallas, Minneapolis, New Orleans and Miami must telephone Washington whenever a ruling was required.[87]

In addition to the problems caused by geography, the vague wording of the restrictions and hence their interpretation by "field censors" caused resentment and confusion for the press and censoring officials alike:

> Oftentimes [sic] generals and admirals were in sharp disagreement as to what should be suppressed or passed, so that rulings flatly contradicted each other. One group of high officials, with some appreciation of publicity values, would urge pictures and features stories, while another group would not want to admit that we had either an army or a navy.[88]

The confusion at the top was duplicated in the field. The regional offices charged with evaluating press material for censorship rulings simply "played safe, ruling against publication even when suppression was patently absurd."[88]

This caused considerable discord among newsmen.
Examples abounded. The censors told publications for
months to avoid photographing tanks, but when an officer
inadvertently permitted a newsreel team to use tank
photographs, the decision was made to allow other
publications to use them. One officer refused to allow
publications to use aircraft photographs while another
officer permitted them.[70] Often the restrictions were
absurd:

> There were many instances where papers were
> denied permission to give the location of aviation
> plants although the information was to be found in
> every telephone and city directory. A powder
> factory was being built in plain view of a large
> city . . but reporters were ordered to ignore its
> existence.[71]

Another problem caused by voluntary censorship was
that some newsmen ignored it. When papers learned of the
content of military testimony before secret congressional
committee sessions, they often couldn't 'resist an
exclusive story.'[72]

Even the report of the arrival of the first
transports containing U.S. forces to France was a subject
of controversy:

> . In order to minimize the danger of submarine
> attacks, our first transports sailed in separated
> detachments, and the papers were asked to print
> nothing until the last of the four groups reached
> France. The Associated Press announced the arrival
> of the first group while the other three were still
> in the danger zone.[73]

Other military censorship missions during the war were the censoring of the mails, telegraph cables, radio and telephone lines which connected the U.S. with other countries. Censorship restrictions, the wartime Espionage Act of 1917 and the Trading With the Enemy Act were used to prevent the publication of many Socialist and German-language publications, to ban dozens of books, to restrict the flow of news from the U.S. through the mail and over international telegraph lines, and to selectively prevent many U.S. publications from being distributed outside the U.S.[74]

More pertinent to the discussion in this thesis, however, are the censorship restrictions placed on correspondents accompanying the American Expeditionary Force, the A.E.F, to France in July 1917. They proved more restrictive than domestic restrictions. Even the accreditation process was restrictive:

> First the correspondent had to appear personally before the Secretary of War or his authorized representative and swear that he would 'convey the truth to the people of the United States' but refrain from disclosing facts which might aid the enemy.[75]

The correspondent had to post a $10,000 bond to be forfeited and given to charity if 'he were sent back for any infraction of the rules.'[76] The correspondents, initially twelve and never numbering above forty, paid from $1,000 to $3,000 to the War Department for their overseas transportation and other expenses.[77]

In contrast to domestic censorship, U.S. censorship in France was involuntary. But one correspondent wrote after the war that there were restrictions on what American correspondents wrote in addition to those imposed by the A.E.F. These self-imposed restrictions probably had a side effect of keeping A.E.F. censorship from becoming even more restrictive. The 'simple credo which none of us realized we were following, but which all of us actually followed' was:

> That all Americans were natural-born fighters.
> That in any engagement between Americans and Germans, the German force was always from 5 to 10 times as large as the American force.
> That it was difficult in our army to keep the wounded from getting up and rushing back into the fighting.
> That lemonade was the popular French drink for American soldiers.
> That next to reaming a German with his bayonet, the American soldier loved best to play with the little French children back of the lines or helped the French farmer get in his wheat.[76]

In addition to these self-imposed restrictions, the correspondents to the A.E.F. in France signed an agreement that they would abide by certain restrictions as a condition of remaining with the A.E.F. The agreement and the censorship restrictions they contained were administered by the Censorship Division of the A.E.F., General Staff's Intelligence Section. The agreement stipulated that:

> The newspaper representative was to submit all correspondence, except personal letters, to the press officer or his assistant (personal letters being censored by the normal mail censors at bases

throughout France]; the correspondent agreed to repeat no information he received at the front unless it had previously passed the censor; he was to give neither the name nor location of any unit; there was to be no revelation of future plans or of any information that Military Intelligence might have thought of value to the enemy; and, the correspondent agreed to accept the press officer's instructions as further censorship rules from time to time . . . If the press representative violated any of these rules, he would be liable to suspension, dismissal with a public reprimand, or detention during the period when some operation was in progress.[79]

Through December 1917, the involuntary restrictions drew criticism from the correspondents but were grudgingly accepted. During the fall of 1917, however, the "accumulation of military and political failures" which the censorship restrictions obscured in U.S. reporters' dispatches was difficult for reporters to accept.[80]

A particular story the U.S. correspondents in France were eager to report but were prevented by War Department censorship policy was the failure of the U.S. and Allies to alleviate the supply shortages which had developed since the A.E.F. arrival in France. Even General Pershing's personal request to the Secretary of War to allow the correspondents to write a "watered-down story on the supply muddle" was rejected. One reporter took desperate action.[81]

To avoid the A.E.F. censorship restrictions, New York *Tribune* reporter Heywood Broun "packed his bags, returned to New York," and wrote articles on the supply blunders. In the ensuing uproar and flurry of calls for

Congressional investigations, he forfeited his #10,000
bond. Pershing considered publicly rebuking him but
settled on revoking his A.E.F. credentials.[82]

A second method used for avoiding censorship
restrictions was mailing stories to the U.S. using the
French international postal system. In early 1918, a
controversial story appeared in the U.S. concerning a new
U.S. gas mask. The story was written in France by a United
Press correspondent who avoided censorship restrictions by
using the intermittently censored French mail system to
file his report. The story caused a furor in Washington
because it described the improvements the mask had over
existing types and identified the nine gases the mask
protected the wearer from. War Department officials were
concerned that 'German chemists would immediately produce a
tenth gas and so render the masks obsolete.' The uproar
was only quieted after it was realized that the 'United
Press had only told the American people what the Germans
learned as soon as they took the first prisoner wearing the
new mask.'[83]

A third attempt to avoid censorship restrictions
was not as successful. United Press reporter Westbrook
Pegler's attempt to smuggle a story out of France was
intercepted by British censors. The story was on the
soldier deaths the unhealthy winter living conditions in
the A.E.F. caused. Pershing requested Pegler's replacement

since 'at twenty-three he was too youthful and
inexperienced,' and the United Press had no choice but to
recall him.[84]

A second reporter had his accreditation to the
A.E.F. revoked for violating censorship restrictions. New
York *Times* reporter Wythe Williams had his credentials
lifted for sending a story to the *Collier's Weekly* without
submitting it to the A.E.F. censor.[85]

In addition to press reports, photographs were
censored by the A.E.F. The censorship restrictions on
photographs were similar to those in place for press
reports. However, the restrictions were more subjective in
that they prohibited images which might have a 'depressing
effect on the public at home' by depicting 'the mangled
remains of a fallen airplane . . . the wreck of a war
vessel . . . a trench of American dead . . . an operating
room in a military hospital' or the 'picking up of
Americans killed in action.'[86]

Though the restrictions were stringent, few
photographs were actually withheld by the censors, though
the routine painting out of details of military
significance left some photographs 'so retouched that they
looked like paintings.'[87]   Of 1,650 photographs examined
in a three month period in 1918, only 56 were held.[88]

By late 1917, the correspondents felt censorship
had become too restrictive. Two examples of the abuses the

reporters felt from the censors had little to do with
military operations. Censors killed a story on several
cases of wine the French presented to the Americans as a
gift because "it suggests bibulous indulgence by American
soldiers which might offend temperance forces in the United
States."[88]

A second example concerned a reporter's cable
requesting reimbursement for expenses incurred while
touring rural France. Since the reporter couldn't remember
where he had spent the money, he wired "Entertaining
General Pershing--$250." The censor refused to send the
cable, saying "it reflected (negatively) on the Commander-
in-Chief."[89]

In addition to what reporters felt were
unreasonable uses of the censorship restrictions, news of
other important events in A.E.F. operations were
suppressed. Reports of the first occupation of a sector of
the front lines by a U.S. division in 1917 were prevented
from being transmitted for seventeen days.[91]

Correspondents on several occasions used clever
manipulations of the censorship system to scoop their
competitors. These scoops only fueled the rage of the
other reporters at the harsh censorship restrictions. When
former President Theodore Roosevelt's son Archie was
wounded in action while serving with the A.E.F., censors
refused to allow the reporters to report the wounding until

an official announcement was made in Washington. One
reporter simply filed a story on Roosevelt's receipt of an
award for heroism during an action in which he was also
wounded, as was acceptable under the censorship
restrictions. The ploy allowed him to slip the report by
the censor.[82]

A second manipulation of the censorship system also
involved former President Theodore Roosevelt and the use of
the French mails. By late 1917, correspondent Reginald
Kauffman of the Philadelphia *North American* developed a
system which avoided A.E.F. censorship. Knowing that
French postal censors only examined about 20 percent of all
letters, and realizing they would be even less likely to
examine letters addressed to a former President of the
United States, he simply arranged with Roosevelt to mail
his reports to him in the U.S. Roosevelt would then write
stories under his own name using Kauffman's information.
Though Army Intelligence investigated Kauffman's activities
"they were not able to interrupt the transmission of his
reports,"[83] and he remained in France. They did, however,
make him the third correspondent to lose both his $10,000
bond and his A.E.F. credentials.[84]

Later in the war, United Press correspondent Fred
Ferguson also used the A.E.F. censorship system to scoop
his competitors. After being briefed with other
correspondents the night before about the hour-by-hour plan

of the September 1918 American attack on the Saint-Mihiel
salient, "while the other correspondents turned in . . .
Ferguson sat down and wrote the story of the battle as if
it had already happened." He wrote the story in short
sections and took the sections to the censor. When
Ferguson and the other reporters left the next morning to
cover the attack, he left the accommodating censor to file
the correct sections of the story which proved accurate as
the attack progressed. The censor sent enough of the
sections out that Ferguson scooped his competitors by
nearly 12 hours.[85]

Censorship restrictions eased in February 1918.
The new restrictions, as did previous restrictions,
prohibited most photography by persons accompanying or
assigned to the A.E.F.[86] and required that correspondents'
reports meet four new conditions:

That they were accurate in statement and
implication, did not supply military information to
the enemy, did not injure the morale of our forces
abroad, at home, or among our Allies, and would not
embarrass the United States or the Allies in
neutral countries.[87]

The new instructions permitted the use of the names
of individual soldiers. Locations where U.S. forces were
operating could be identified after the "enemy had
established this fact by taking prisoners."[88]

The new restrictions did nothing to prevent the
worst mistake any correspondent made in the war: the
premature announcement of the armistice. A United Press

correspondent visiting the commander of U.S. naval forces in France was told the American Embassy had announced the armistice had been signed. The correspondent promptly reported the story, not realizing the announcement was a hoax. Unfortunately for the United Press, the French telegraph operator assumed the report had been reviewed by the censor and sent it to the world without verifying its validity. The publishing of the report and a subsequent United Press retraction caused heaping criticism to be poured on both the censorship system and the United Press. The signing of the armistice three days later had "something of the edge taken off the jubilation."[99]

The final revision of A.E.F. press censorship regulations came shortly after the armistice. The new restrictions allowed individuals and units to be identified specifically but prohibited criticism of the continued U.S. presence in Europe or the discussion of the return of U.S. troops to America. One regulation of interest was that:

> There would be no publication of articles on atrocities unless the facts had been investigated with the greatest care, and would be able to stand the same test as would be applied to them in a court proceeding.[100]

In January 1919, the last A.E.F. press censorship restrictions were lifted.[101] On 18 June 1919, the final censorship legacy of World War I, U.S. domestic censorship over the international telegraph cable, was removed.[102]

Conclusions

Press censorship in the Spanish-American War was primarily directed at the transmission of news reports over transoceanic cables, reports which might have provided the Spanish with military intelligence. As the war ended, however censorship in the Philippines evolved more into a method to prevent criticism of the conduct of the counterinsurgency effort than an effort to protect military secrets. This attitude followed the U.S. armed forces during their Mexican interventions in the early 1900s and characterized the censorship restrictions imposed by the U.S. there.

Upon the U.S. entry into World War I, the Committee for Public Information began a two-pronged effort to sell the war to the American people and to protect military secrets in the continental U.S. through voluntary press censorship. The voluntary press censorship was enforced for the most part by military officers. It proved less restrictive than the involuntary censorship restrictions placed on press reports and photographs coming from correspondents accompanying the American Expeditionary Force in France. Correspondents imposed their own restrictions on the tone of their reporting which probably kept A.E.F. censorship from becoming even more restrictive. These correspondents chafed under the involuntary A.E.F. restrictions and repeatedly circumvented them to report stories they felt were suppressed for purely political

reasons.

CHAPTER 3 ENDNOTES

1. Robert Leckie, *The Wars of America* (New York: Harper and Row, 1981), p. 547.

2. Charles H. Brown, *The Correspondents' War: Journalists in the Spanish American War* (New York: Charles Scribner's Sons, 1967), pp. 117-21.

3. Ibid., p. 119.

4. Ibid., p. 189.

5. Ibid.

6. Leckie, pp. 547-48.

7. F. Lauriston Bullard, *Famous War Correspondents* (Boston: Little, Brown and Co., 1914), p. 413.

8. Leckie, p. 551.

9. Brown, p. 225.

10. U.S. War Department, *Annual Report of the War Department for the Fiscal Year Ending June 30, 1898. Report of the Chiefs of Bureaus* (Washington, D.C.: U.S. Government Printing Office, 1898), p. 215; and Brown, p. 226.

11. Brown, pp. 213-14.

12. Ibid., pp. 215-20.

13. Report of the Secretary of War, Fiscal Year 1898, pp. 966-967; and Brown, pp. 225-227.

14. Brown, p. 227.

15. James R. Mock, *Censorship 1917* (Princeton, NJ: Princeton University Press, 1941), p. 18; and Byron Price, "Governmental Censorship in Wartime," *The American Political Science Review*, (36, No. 5, October 1942): 839.

16. Ibid.

17. Brown, p. 228.

18. Report of the Secretary of War, Fiscal Year 1898, p. 966.

19. Brown, p. 269.

20. Report of the Secretary of War, Fiscal Year 1898, p. 966.

21. Brown, p. 269.

22. Ibid., p. 266.

23. Ibid., p. 237.

24. U.S. War Department, *Annual Report of the War Department for the Fiscal Year Ending June 30, 1899. Report of the Chiefs of Bureaus* (Washington, D.C.: U.S. Government Printing Office, 1899), p. 737.

25. Brown, p. 270.

26. Mott, pp. 536-37.

27. Brown, p. 430.

28. Ibid., p. 435.

29. Ibid., p. 435.

30. Bullard, pp. 416-17.

31. Brown, p. 420.

32. Ibid.

33. William Manchester, *American Caesar: Douglas MacArthur 1880-1964* (New York: Dell, 1978), pp. 42-43, and Leckie, p. 570; and Richard E. Welch, Jr., *Response to Imperialism-- The United States and the Philippine-American War, 1899- 1902* (Chapel Hill, NC: University of North Carolina Press, 1979), p. 134.

34. Stuart C. Miller, *Benevolent Assimilation--The American Conquest of the Philippines, 1899-1903* (New Haven, Conn.: Yale University Press, 1982) p. 83.

35. Leon Wolff, *Little Brown Brothers--How the United States Purchased and Pacified the Philippine Islands at the Century's Turn* (New York: Doubleday,1961), p. 261.

36. Ibid.

37. Miller, p. 84.

38. Ibid.

39. Ibid., p. 85.

40. Wolff, pp. 262-63.

41. Mock, p. 19.

42. Miller, p. 82.

43. Ibid.

44. Wolff, p. 265.

45. Miller, p. 86.

46. Ibid., pp. 86-87.

47. James H. Blount, *The American Occupation of the Philippines 1898-1912* (New York: Putnam& Sons, 1912), p. 222.

48. Miller, p. 99.

49. Leckie, p. 571.

50. Report of the Secretary of War, Fiscal Year 1899, p. 801.

51. Mock, p. 20.

52. Ibid., p. 165.

53. Ibid., p. 20.

54. Ibid., p. 21.

55. Ibid., pp. 21-22.

56. Ibid.

57. Manchester, p. 90.

58. Robert E. Summers, ed., *Wartime Censorship of Press and Radio* (New York: H. W. Wilson, 1942), p. 67.

59. Mock, pp. 40-49.

60. Ibid.

61. James R. Wiggins, *Freedom or Secrecy* (New York: Oxford University Press, 1964), p. 95.

62. Summers, p. 67.

63. Ibid., p. 68.

64. Mott, p. 626.

65. Edwin & Michael Emery, *The Press and America: An Interpretative History*, 5th ed., (Englewood Cliffs, N.J.: Prentice Hall, 1984), p. 357.

66. Summers, p. 70.

67. Ibid., p. 71.

68. Ibid.

69. Ibid.

70. Ibid.

71. Ibid., p. 71.

72. Ibid.

73. Ibid., p. 73.

74. Mock, pp. 43-169.

75. Phillip Knightley, *The First Casualty* (New York: Harcourt, Brace, Jovanovich, 1976), p. 124.

76. Ibid.

77. Ibid. and M. L. Stein, *Under Fire--The Story of American War Correspondents* (New York: Julian Messner, 1968), p. 70.

78. Stein, p. 71.

79. Mock, p. 103.

80. Emmet Crozier, *American Reporters on the Western Front 1914-1918* (New York: Oxford University Press, 1959), p. 160.

81. Ibid., pp. 181-82.

82. Ibid., pp. 183-91.

83. Ibid., p. 229.

84. Knightley, p. 130.

85. Ibid., pp. 196-97.

86. Susan D. Moeller, *Shooting War* (New York: Basic Books, 1989), p. 114.

87. Ibid., p. 217.

88. Ibid., p. 431.

89. Ibid.

90. Crozier, p. 159.

91. Ibid., pp. 189-90.

92. Knightley, p. 132.

93. Crozier, p. 178.

94. Ibid., p. 192.

95. Knightley, p. 133.

96. Mock, p. 105.

97. Ibid., p. 104.

98. Ibid.

99. Mott, pp. 630-31; and Crozier, pp. 260-67.

100. Mock, p. 104.

101. Ibid., p. 105.

102. Ibid., p. 92.

CHAPTER 4

U.S. WARTIME PRESS CENSORSHIP IN WORLD WAR II

Wartime press censorship in World War II began
immediately after the Japanese attack on Pearl Harbor,
Hawaii, on December 7, 1941. Radio, telegraph cable, and
mail censorship by military personnel began immediately
after the attack in the U.S. and its territories. Losses
and other details of the attack were not allowed to be sent
from Hawaii by correspondents for months and many of the
specifics about the U.S. defeat were first reported in New
York and Washington with information from sources there.[1]

The conduct of World War II U.S. press censorship
was characterized by location: voluntary domestic press
censorship in the continental U.S., somewhat restrictive
involuntary censorship in the European theater of
operations, and highly restrictive involuntary censorship
in the Pacific theaters of operations.

Voluntary Domestic Censorship

Voluntary domestic censorship began even before the
U.S. officially entered the war. An attempt to prevent the

71

Germans from learning about British lend-lease shipping and
U.S. support to British convoys in 1940 proved ineffective:

> In December 1940, Secretary of the Navy Frank Knox
> asked editors and broadcasters to withhold . . .
> news about British ships in American ports. That
> was too much, for thousands of people could see the
> ships, and an enemy agent could freely send the
> news out of the country . . . [since] international
> channels of communication [were] open.[2]

From the moment of the Japanese attack on Pearl
Harbor, however, `editors looked to the White House for
some hint as to whether a compulsory (domestic) censorship
program would be forthcoming.`[3] The answer was not long in
coming. Though tight restrictions were placed on domestic
radio broadcasts which could be received outside the U.S.,
the voluntary domestic press censorship practices of World
War I were continued.[4] President Franklin Roosevelt issued
the following statement:

> All Americans abhor censorship, just as they
> abhor war. But the experience of this and of all
> other nations has demonstrated that some degree of
> censorship is essential in wartime, and we are at
> war.
> The important thing now is that such forms of
> censorship as are necessary shall be administered
> effectively and in harmony with the best interests
> of our free institutions.
> It is necessary to the national security that
> military information which might be of aid to the
> enemy be scrupulously withheld at the source.
> It is necessary that a watch be set upon our
> borders, so that no such information may reach the
> enemy, inadvertently or otherwise, through the
> medium of the mails, radio or cable transmission,
> or by any other means.
> It is necessary that prohibitions against the
> domestic publication of some types of information,
> contained in long-distance statutes, be rigidly
> enforced.

Finally, the government has called upon a
patriotic press and radio to abstain voluntarily
from the dissemination of detailed information of
certain kinds, such as reports of the movements of
vessels and troops. The response has indicated a
universal desire to cooperate.

In order that all of these parallel and
requisite undertakings may be coordinated and
carried forward in accordance with a single uniform
policy, I have appointed Byron Price, executive
news editor of the Associated Press, to be the
Director of Censorship, responsible directly to the
President.⁵

Price's Office of Censorship was based on "20 years

of study by a Joint Army-Navy Committee" and was created

"when the President adopted, with minor revisions, the

Army-Navy censorship plan."⁶ The Office eventually had a

staff of nearly 16,000 military and civilian personnel

censoring both U.S. media and the mails.⁷ The Office

continued operations throughout the war, closing down on 15

August 1945, hours after the Japanese surrender.⁸

Domestic censorship remained voluntary throughout

the war with military officers in regional censorship

offices providing "advice" to print and broadcast newsmen.

Price recorded his views on censorship which guided this

"advice" during the war:

Censorship is a war measure. It is justifiable
only in so far as it aids prosecution of the war.
Censorship is no respecter of persons. No one is
exempt. But censorship does respect the mails and
the cables. Censorship is frank with the public.
Rules and reasons for them are published, for
prevention in censorship is much better than cure.
The best censorship, if any censorship can be so
called, is one of facts rather than opinion. The
key to suppressing information is whether it would
help the enemy.⁹

If a reporter, however, failed to seek the 'advice' or if it was ignored, dire consequences could follow. Chicago *Tribune* reporter Stanley Johnston transited the Pacific in June 1942 and learned of the Battle of Midway from conversations with U.S. sailors. Using a short Navy communique on some of the details of the battle and the Japanese losses, he and another reporter used *Jane's Fighting Ships* and roughed out the likely compositions of the two opposing fleets . . . and wrote 'with remarkable accuracy, an account' of the battle. The reporters 'were immediately summoned to Washington and interrogated by Navy Department officials' and were nearly indicted by a special federal grand jury for violating the Espionage Act.[10]

Johnston's name and the nature of the investigation were revealed and despite his being exonerated, the damage to his reputation was done. After the war, Johnston learned the reason for the government's harsh handling of his case. The Navy feared (wrongly) that the Japanese would deduce from the accuracy of his article that the U.S. had broken Japanese naval codes. Ignoring the 'voluntary' domestic censorship 'advice' proved costly to Johnston.[11]

Byron Price's Office of Censorship issued a Press Code and a Radio code in January 1942, both of which remained in effect throughout the war to provide the basis for the voluntary censorship guidelines. U.S. forces in theaters of operation used the codes as guidelines for their involuntary censorship reviews, together with local theater and war department supplements.[12] In addition, the National Association of Broadcasters issued a War Service Bulletin and a Wartime Guide in December 1941 to provide additional voluntary and involuntary censorship guidelines for radio broadcasts. These documents are contained in Appendix 2.

Wartime press censorship by the U.S. armed forces in World War II was a massive undertaking involving thousands of military personnel directly engaged in censoring correspondents' copy in theaters of operation or providing voluntary domestic censorship 'advice.' The effectiveness of World War II censorship measures was similar to that of World War I: tight censorship in the theater of operations, haphazard at home.

A typical case involved radio commentator Drew Pearson and General George Patton's famous 'slapping incident.' When Patton was forced by General Dwight Eisenhower to apologize to two combat fatigued soldiers he had slapped for 'feigning illness,' correspondents in the European theater were 'asked' to 'suppress the story.' Though the suppression of the story generated dissent in Europe, the correspondents complied. Three months after the incident, Washington columnist Drew Pearson learned of the story and reported it on his radio show. Before the broadcast, when he requested 'advice' as to whether the story violated voluntary censorship guidelines, Pearson was told by the Office of Censorship that the story could be used only over the objections of the War Department. The War Department had 'urged that the story be withheld, not on grounds of security but for reasons of 'morale.'' Pearson used the story anyway.[13]

Even after the Pearson report, censors in Europe continued to hold the story until 'Eisenhower's staff issued a statement.' A short time later the story was cleared and though it was nearly four months old made headlines throughout the world.[14]

The controversy over the 'slapping incident' had an effect on the censorship policy for a similar event in Burma. A U.S. regimental-sized unit, Merrill's Marauders, had attacked Japanese forces in Burma to 'secure the trace for an overland route' through Burma to China.[15] After the attack faltered, a request for reinforcements resulted in an number of ambulatory hospital patients from the unit being ordered to board aircraft to be transported to join in the attack. Many of the men were 'skeletons from malaria, dysentery and other ailments' and they believed 'not one of them would live long in the jungle.' After marching to the aircraft,' instead of climbing aboard, they threw down their rifles and refused to go. They talked of killing . . .' their commander and of 'deserting en masse.'

The soldiers returned to the hospital, where they eventually received an apology from Merrill himself.[16]

When Associated Press correspondent Relman Morin filed a story on the incident, the censor refused to pass the report. Using the argument that the "army had been unable to bottle up the Patton slapping story" and that the soldiers involved would soon rotate to the U.S. and no longer be subject to censorship, Morin convinced the censor to allow the story to pass. Bereft of the "slapping incident's" stigma of "cover-up," the Burma incident raised no furor.[17]

Censorship in the European Theater of Operations

Prior to the arrival of U.S. forces in the European theater, the War Department evaluated British censorship policies to determine the form U.S. censorship in the theater would take. The evaluation found several factors. First, the French and the British governments independently censored their own correspondents. Second, there was no formal agreement between the two allies on censorship procedures. Finally, the British had adopted a voluntary censorship program in the British Isles similar to U.S. domestic censorship in which:

> . . . by submitting articles for publication to the
> [British] Ministry of Information censorship,
> editors were absolved from any legal action that
> might result from a breach of security in the
> published material. If the submission was
> "stopped," the editor could, under the system,
> publish the article anyway.[18]

Based on the evaluation, the War Department policy
became one of independence from the British. U.S. military
censors from the Allied Expeditionary Force headquarters
intelligence section (and later public relations
officers)[19] would censor correspondents accredited by the
U.S. No formal agreement was reached with the British,
though material of interest to the British was routinely
forwarded by U.S. censors to British censors and vice
versa. Censorship coordination remained informal
throughout the war.[20]

Correspondents accredited by the U.S. were subject
to military discipline or expulsion from the theater of war
if they violated censorship restrictions.[21]

Initially operating in London, censorship officials
deployed to Gibraltar and then North Africa in 1942 to
support the operations in the Mediterranean. The censors,
known as field press censors, received for clearance
"articles by accredited correspondents, scripts and records
for broadcast, photographs, drawings, films, material from
serving personnel (soldiers in the theater), and press
handouts."[22]

The material could be marked in three ways:
"passed," "passed as cut," or "held." As Allied operations
continued, the "Bible" of censorship guidance, civilian
technical journals, previously cleared information,
communiques, condensed enemy news reports, and other

supplementary censorship guidance increased in size. These documents eventually exceeded 200 pages.[23] When faced with this volume of information, and to prevent 'dual' censorship (censorship in the field and in London), the main U.S. censorship effort in Europe remained centralized in two locations. They remained for most of the war collocated with the Supreme Headquarters Allied Expeditionary Force (SHAEF) and the U.S. Eighth Air Force headquarters, staging forward to the Mediterranean and to France as operations progressed.[24]

When Allied armies deployed to North Africa, Italy, and France, field press censors accompanied them. These censors could clear copy for 'fighting which was taking place within the bounds' of their army or army group. Reports on any other subject had to be cleared by SHAEF or Eighth Air Force censors.[25]

As the Allied armies advanced into Germany, the stories censored by SHAEF alone from January to April 1945 contained more than 25 million words.[26] These stories were censored by dozens of temporarily assigned personnel and nearly 200 permanently assigned commissioned and noncommissioned officers.[27]

In general, censorship in the European theater was effective, and was not viewed as excessively harsh by U.S. correspondents. The complaints that did occur centered on alleged political censorship or censorship of criticism, an

absence of a sense of urgency on the part of the censors,
resulting in slow processing of copy, or on the delay of
stories from one correspondent while other stories were
cleared on the same subject. Another complaint was the
correspondents' perception of a general lack of knowledge
of the news business and the armed forces on the part of
the censors.[28] Often, these complaints simply resulted
from the SHAEF censorship office releasing 'held' stories
immediately upon the declassification of an operation and
then informing army and army group censors they could
release 'held' stories on the same operation. The
resultant delays for correspondents' stories at army and
army group level gave SHAEF correspondents a scoop over
their competitors in the field.[29]

Typical of the charges of political censorship was
General Eisenhower's decision to censor discussion of Vichy
French Admiral Darlan's retention as ranking French
official following the Allied invasion of North Africa.
Eisenhower's concern was to prevent 'the delicate
situation' the Allies faced in North Africa from being
'made even more difficult.'[30] Though the retention of
Darlan was beneficial to the Allied cause, the decision
'brought criticism from those who objected to a
collaborationist remaining in power.'[31]

The criticism against the controversial decision to
retain Darlan was quickly joined by criticism of the

censorship ban on discussing it in the press.[32]

Correspondents were incensed:

> It was difficult for correspondents to see how
> this project [the North African invasion] could
> have been either impeded or endangered by
> permitting them to report the political situation
> in North Africa, ominous as it may have been
> Censoring the story was an error, as General
> Eisenhower admitted.[33]

A second controversial case of political censorship was the decision to suppress stories on the prevention of the U.S. Army from advancing to Berlin in May 1945 before the Russians could do so. Though President Truman approved "General Eisenhower's recommendation that for military considerations the Americans should stop their advance at the Elbe and leave the capture of Berlin to the Russians," the correspondents in Europe loudly decried the decision to stifle comment.[34]

The censorship policies on two significant events during the war in Europe were similar. For several days after the U.S. defeat at Kasserine Pass in North Africa in 1943, and for several days after the German counter-offensive in the Ardennes in 1944-1945, a censorship blackout was imposed. In both cases:

> . . . the blackout was interpreted (by
> correspondents) as a SHAEF device to withhold bad
> news and, consequently, imaginations of mothers and
> fathers and sweethearts were running wild.[35]

Despite this concern, SHAEF retained the temporary blackouts to prevent the Germans from learning of Allied troop movements so they 'could better plan their tactics.'[36]

The handling of the biggest story of the war in Europe, the invasion of France, was typical of SHAEF censorship policies. Correspondents were briefed by SHAEF staff briefers and by General Eisenhower personally on the details of the operation. Correspondents knew the particulars of the operation, yet respected the censorship:

> Prior to D-Day, public relations officers and censors met jointly with correspondents outlining what could be passed and what could not . . . when the *Saturday Evening Post's* man turned in his story of some 5,000 words immediately after launching of the operation, only one word had to be eliminated or changed. *Colliers'* story . . . passed without a single change.[37]

Most of the criticism of censorship in Europe resulted from the process in which correspondents 'negotiated' clearance of their material. Correspondents routinely had access to classified and sensitive material on Allied operations and weapons systems. If a correspondent could convince a censor of the innocuous nature of his or her dispatch, the censor would pass it, while simultaneously another correspondent's story containing the same material would be held by a different censor. Often, the correspondent convinced censors to clear information which violated security guidelines.

In one violation, a technical journal wrote a story in Britain on the B-29 *Superfortress* and provided it to the

Eighth Air Force censor for clearance, claiming its source
of information to be already cleared U.S. press reports:

> The article began: "It may now be revealed from
> information in the American press that . . ." This
> article, widely reprinted, gave dimensions, speed,
> carrying capacity and range of the B-29 in December
> 1943, a year before the first B-29 reached a
> theater of war. It was passed by an Air Censor
> whose most dependable guidance on what could or
> could not be said about the *Superfortress* was the
> written word of the magazine submitting.[38]

By far the most glaring censorship failure of World
War II was the premature announcement of the signing of the
peace treaty which ended the war in Europe. Stalin had
demanded that the "victory announcement should come
simultaneously from the chiefs of all the Allied
nations."[39] Associated Press correspondent Edward Kennedy
and the other correspondents who witnessed the signing
were:

> . . . pledged not to release their stories until an
> officially prescribed time. Kennedy, angered by
> the news that the German radio was announcing the
> surrender in advance of the time set by American,
> British and Russian political leaders, made an
> unauthorized phone call and dictated part of his
> story for transmission. The AP thus had the
> official story of the German surrender a day in
> advance of VE day.[40]

The story was then broadcast throughout the world.
Kennedy's colleagues charged him with committing "the most
disgraceful, deliberate, and unethical double-cross in the
history of journalism."[41] SHAEF suspended the Associated
Press from all activities in the theater, albeit

temporarily, and pulled Kennedy's accreditation. Kennedy

was eventually fired by the AP over the incident.[42]

The Effects of Technology on World War II Censorship

World War II radio and cable telephone and

telegraph technology significantly improved the

transmission time for news stories over those processed in

World War I. In World War I, most stories were mailed to

be published in newspapers and periodicals in the U.S.

Only the hottest stories of World War I were telegraphed to

the U.S. over the transatlantic cable. To carry press

dispatches in World War II, high speed telegraphy and

telephoto technology existed, as did both cable and radio

transatlantic telephones and telegraphs, and non-stop

transatlantic dispatch aircraft.[43]

In addition, throughout World War II radio

technology allowed live broadcasts from the European

theater:

> The wire recorder soon came into use for close-up
> stories of actual combat . . . The networks
> employed international pickups, with more and more
> newscasts directly from the [mainly European] war
> theaters in 1943-44. On the unconditional
> surrender of Italy in September, 1943, General
> Eisenhower himself broadcast the news [live] to the
> world.[44]

World War II radio broadcasting and newspaper

competition resulted in a demand for speedy censorship and

routine immediate transmission of reports to the U.S. For

the most part, these transmissions were made by Western

Union telegraph or by two commercial radio companies: Press

Wireless, and Mackay Radio and Telegraph. Press Wireless,
for example, operated a radio station connecting
correspondents in the Normandy beachhead with their editors
in the United States.[45] Army signal units supplemented the
commercial radio circuits and also periodically provided
direct radio links between correspondents accompanying U.S.
forces in Europe with their editors in the U.S. Stories
transmitted over these direct links were censored by
military officers operating from army and army group
headquarters.[46]

The demand for speed was so great that early in the
war the Associated Press installed a teletype in both the
SHAEF censorship office and the Western Union cable office.
The teletype would simultaneously send identical copy to
both Western Union and the SHAEF censors. When a dispatch
was censored, the censor would call Western Union and
either pass the story or delete the offensive portions.[47]

The improvement in camera and photographic
technology over that of World War I resulted in an
incredible number of photographs and film required to be
censored. In addition, using radio and cable telephoto
systems, photographs were brought "to the news desk along
with the copy."[48] A policy change from World War I
restrictions was that photographs picturing dead Americans
were cleared by censors. The U.S. government in mid-1943
"decided that the time had come for Americans to see the

reality behind the carved names on sun-dappled monuments in hometowns across the country."[48] The pictures could have been gruesome, but while explicit:

> They were pretty restrained given what could have been pictured. The photographs did not show the same devastation that the men at the front saw. There were no dismembered carcasses, there were no faces with hunks missing, and no eyeballs with flies crawling out of them.[50]

Initially, all photographs and film in the theater were censored in an identical manner by the same censors, whether they were official, press or amateur (taken by individual soldiers). The censorship process involved developing the film, printing either photographs or motion picture film, and then censoring the product. Censored official or press photographs were stamped in a similar manner as news stories: "passed," "passed as censored," or "held." The average censorship workload for official and press material was more than 400,000 photographic prints and 35,000 feet of movie film per week.[51]

These procedures were followed until 1944. The amount of film then surpassed the capability of the censors to process it, creating a backlog of amateur film (the lowest priority) of more than 100,000 rolls by mid-1944. The SHAEF censors in July 1944 returned the rolls to the owners and passed the amateur film development responsibility to the Army Exchange Service, who in theory also received the censorship responsibility. The Exchange censorship program proved significantly less effective than the SHAEF program. In reality, unless amateur film or photographs were mailed to the U.S. (and were subjected to the same unit-level censorship soldier mail received), an amateur photographer could photograph any subject with his personal camera and have the film developed and printed without any effective censorship restrictions.[52]

When press or official photographs were censored, they were occasionally retouched by having "street signs," division patches, "and uniform name tags indetectably brushed out . . . (while) other pictures had indistinctly hazed-out features of the dead."[53] More often, photographs were censored by a "flat gray bar or a flat gray field . . . (covering) any objectionable portions of the image."[54]

Censorship in the Pacific Theaters of Operation

While wartime press censorship in Europe was only somewhat restrictive, censorship in the Pacific theaters of operations was highly restrictive. The main reason for the highly restrictive censorship was the control by the military over all means of communication. While civilian radio, telephone and telegraph circuits connected Europe with the U.S., except in Australia and Manila no such links existed in the Pacific theaters.[55]

Another cause of the tight censorship, at least until late 1943, was that the U.S. was losing the war. The government tried to "soften the impact of the frightening

and humiliating defeats at the hands of the Japanese . . .
and to play down losses of men and ships incurred in the
Pearl Harbor attack and in the early Pacific fighting."[56]

For example, press reports from the beleaguered
Philippines were restricted from leaving the island of
Corregidor.[57] The details of U.S. and Japanese losses in
the naval battles of the Coral Sea and Midway were censored
for months after the battles. Stories on the series of
attacks by German and Japanese submarines on the
continental U.S. were suppressed, as were stories on a
Japanese campaign to start forest fires in the northwestern
U.S. by flying incendiary bombs on balloons from Japan.[58]

A third reason for the tight censorship in the
Pacific, at least in the Southwest Pacific Theater, was the
correspondents' perception that General Douglas
"MacArthur's information officers insisted unduly on
personal glorification of the commander."[59] One of
MacArthur's deputies agreed and said MacArthur's public
relations officers felt that:

> . . . unless a news release painted the General
> with a halo and seated him on the highest pedestal
> in the universe, it should be killed. No news
> except favorable news, reflecting complete credit
> on an infallible MacArthur had much chance of
> getting by.[60]

It can be argued that MacArthur's public statements
disagreed with his subordinates' view. Upon his 1942
arrival in Australia from Corregidor he said:

> Men will not fight and men will not die unless
> they know what they are fighting for . . . In
> democracies it is essential that the public know
> the truth.[1]

In practice, however, truth did not always win out.
Following the U.S. return to the Philippines, MacArthur
announced that the capital, Manila, had fallen to U.S.
troops. Due to MacArthur's tight censorship,
correspondents "couldn't expose his victory communique as a
lie--the fall of the capitol was a month away."[2]

Discussion of Pacific Theater Censorship

The debate over censoring the balloon bomb campaign
is representative of the issue of World War II press
censorship in general. One author felt the suppression of
the story prevented the Japanese from enlarging the
campaign:

> What the Japanese needed was information. Were
> the bombs landing? Where? When? Was there any
> damage? They did not get it . . . the balloon
> landings became part of the news that did not
> happen, and the Japanese were not able to learn
> what was going on across the Pacific.[3]

Another author felt the opposite, arguing that the
285 balloons reported as having reached the U.S. out of
9,300 launched was such a poor record that had the Japanese
known they would have cancelled the program.[4] Because of
the censorship "the effect of Japan's 'secret weapon' had
been kept secret from its originators--and it was a dud."
In addition, the author argued that "the time-honored need
for newspapers to quell rumors and prevent panic" was

clearly present in the public panic caused by the balloon bomb campaign.[85]

The rationale for censorship of several stories in the Pacific theaters which incensed correspondents was only explained after the war. Several successes of U.S. forces in the Pacific resulted from the breaking of the Japanese naval code. The stories which were suppressed due to the fear that the Japanese would learn of the U.S. ability to read their coded messages included: the ambush of the airplane carrying the Japanese planner of the Pearl Harbor attack, Admiral Yamamoto, and the U.S. victory at Midway.[86]

Another case of censorship which was only explained after the war was the suppression of the success of U.S. submarines and their relative invulnerability to Japanese depth charge tactics:

> 'We wanted him [the Japanese] to think . . . that every time he dropped a depth charge, another submarine went to Davy Jones' locker.' Repeated stories of successes of our submarines . . . and exploits identifiable with any particular submarine would have helped him evaluate what he was doing wrong.[87]

Other cases of censorship which were only explained after the war were suppression of stories on the kamikaze suicide planes damaging Allied ships, of the successes of the U.S. navy underwater demolition teams in clearing beaches of obstacles before amphibious assaults, and of the prohibition of interviews with Japanese prisoners.[88]

90

Censoring the effects of the kamikazes kept the
Japanese from learning of their effectiveness:

> . . . when the suicide pilots started descending on
> our ships, complete 'stops' were issued indicating
> loss or damaging of our vessels. The pilot who was
> successful in his mission did not return. Higher
> authority who sent him on his perilous task had no
> way of knowing whether he succeeded or failed
> unless we informed him.**

Censoring the successes of the U.S. navy underwater

demolition teams in clearing beaches of obstacles before

amphibious assaults drew criticism from correspondents, but

was justified by evidence gathered after the war. Japanese

commanders defending against amphibious attacks rarely

reported accurately the employment by the U.S. of

underwater demolition teams. This failure combined with

the suppression of word of the tactic from news reports

prevented adequate Japanese defenses from being deployed

against future assaults. Had the reports been cleared 'our

underwater demolition men would have met murderous

reception on their subsequent swim-ins. As it was, their

casualty rate was but a fraction of what had been

feared.'70

Another point of criticism of Pacific theater

censorship was the ban on publishing interviews with

Japanese prisoners. Since Japanese soldiers were never

expected to become prisoners, they were not told to avoid

giving information to their captors. Many Japanese

prisoners did provide much useful information to the Allies

and the Allied leadership wanted to prevent the Japanese from changing their ˙viewpoint in this regard by starting to indoctrinate Japanese soldiers against talking in the event of capture.˙ No reports of the readiness of Japanese prisoners to provide information to the Allies were cleared until the end of the war.[71]

Conclusions on World War II Censorship

The record of U.S. wartime press censorship in World War II was impressive:

> It kept war production efforts secret until they
> had reached safe levels, kept Germany uninformed of
> the near-success of her submarine blockade on 1942,
> suppressed all hints of preparations for the
> invasion landings in North Africa and Normandy,
> kept silence about Presidential tours, . . .
> preserved the early development of radar and the
> preparation of the atomic bomb.[72]

Overall, wartime press censorship by the U.S. armed forces in World War II was characterized by voluntary censorship at home and involuntary censorship in the theaters of war. In almost all cases, the media respected both types of censorship. The advent of transoceanic radio, telephone and telephoto technology forever changed how subsequent wars would be reported. The ˙real time˙ reporting capability of the new technology placed a burden of immediacy on censors which would affect censorship policies of the Korean War.

CHAPTER 4 ENDNOTES

1. Byron Price, "Governmental Censorship in Wartime," *The American Political Science Review*, (36, No. 5, October 1942): 842; James R. Mock, George Creel, Neville Miller, Zechariah Chafee, Jr., Ralph Casey, and Arthur Krock. "The Limits of Censorship: A Symposium." *Public Opinion Quarterly*, Spring 1942, p. 25; M. L. Stein, *Under Fire--The Story of American War Correspondents* (New York: Julian Messner, 1968), p. 106; and Patrick S. Washburn, *A Question of Sedition: The Federal Government's Investigation of the Black Press During World War II* (New York: Oxford University Press, 1986), p. 47.

2. Theodore F. Koop, "We Need to Know." *Air Force* (38, No. 10, October 1955): 50.

3. Theodore F. Koop, *Weapon of Silence* (Chicago: University of Chicago Press, 1946), p. 163.

4. U.S. President, Executive Order, "Executive Order Creating Communications Board," 10 December 1941, quoted in Robert E. Summers, ed., *Wartime Censorship of Press and Radio* (New York: H. W. Wilson, 1942), pp. 253-55.

5. U.S. President, statement to the press, 16 December 1941, quoted in Robert E. Summers, ed., *Wartime Censorship of Press and Radio* (New York: H. W. Wilson, 1942), pp. 95-96.

6. U.S. Department of the Army, *History of Military Mobilization in the United States Army 1775-1945 (Department of the Army Pamphlet 20-212)*, Washington, D.C., November 1954, p. 616.

7. Price, p. 842.

8. Koop, *Weapon of Silence*, p. 283.

9. Price, p. 849.

10. Phillip Knightley, *The First Casualty*, (New York: Harcourt, Brace, Jovanovich, 1976), pp. 283-84.

11. Ibid.

12. U.S. 201st Field Press Censorship Organization, History of United States and Supreme Headquarters Allied Expeditionary Force Press Censorship in the European Theater of Operations, 1942-1945, *Paramus, NJ, 1953, p. 9.*

13. *Koop, Weapon of Silence*, p. 261; and Richard W. Steele, "News of the 'Good War': World War II News Management." *Journalism Quarterly* (62, No. 4, Winter 1985): 716.

14. Knightley, p. 321.

15. John Elsberg, ed., *American Military History* (Washington, D.C.: Center of Military History, U.S. Army, 1989), p. 521.

16. Kent Cooper, *The Right to Know: An Exposition of the Evils of News Suppression and Propaganda* (New York: Farrar, Straus and Cudahy, 1956), pp. 195-96.

17. Ibid., p. 196.

18. U.S. 201st Field Press Censorship Organization, History of United States and Supreme Headquarters Allied Expeditionary Force Press Censorship in the European Theater of Operations, 1942-1945, p. 2.

19. Office of the Deputy Chief Signal Officer, Supreme Headquarters Allied Expeditionary Force. "Press Communications." Letter to Chief Signal Officer, War Department, France, 1944, p. 4.

20. Ibid., pp. 1-3.

21. Stein, 148, and Lieutenant Colonel Melvin B. Voorhees, U.S. Army, *Korean Tales* (New York: Simon and Schuster, 1952), p. 111.

22. U.S. 201st Field Press Censorship Organization, History of United States and Supreme Headquarters Allied Expeditionary Force Press Censorship in the European Theater of Operations, 1942-1945, p. 9.

23. Ibid., p. 19.

24. Ibid., pp. 10-12.

25. Ibid., pp. 40-41.

26. Ibid., p. 52.

27. Ibid., p. 46.

28. Ibid., p. 20.

29. Ibid., p. 107.

30. Koop, *Weapon of Silence*, pp. 252-53.

31. Ibid., p. 252.

32. Stephen E. Ambrose, *Eisenhower--Soldier, General of the Army, President-Elect 1890-1952* (New York: Simon and Schuster, 1983), pp. 208-9.

33. Kent Cooper, *The Right to Know: An Exposition of the Evils of News Suppression and Propaganda* (New York: Farrar, Straus and Cudahy, 1956), p. 202.

34. Cooper, pp. 202-5.

35. Captain Harry C. Butcher, U.S. Naval Reserve, *My Three Years with Eisenhower* (New York: Simon and Schuster, 1946), pp. 729-31.

36. Ibid.

37. Commander Harold B. Say, U.S. Naval Reserve, "Censorship and Security." *Proceedings*, (79, No. 2 February 1953): 139.

38. U.S. 201st Field Press Censorship Organization, History of United States and Supreme Headquarters Allied Expeditionary Force Press Censorship in the European Theater of Operations, 1942-1945, p. 95.

39. Frank L. Mott, *American Journalism, A History: 1690-1960* (Toronto: MacMillan and Company, 1969), p. 758.

40. Edwin and Michael Emery, *The Press and America: An Interpretative History*, 5th ed., (Englewood Cliffs, Prentice Hall, 1984), p. 480.

41. Mott, p. 758.

42. Ibid.

43. Office of the Deputy Chief Signal Officer, Supreme Headquarters Allied Expeditionary Force, "Press Communications," p. 38.

44. Mott, p. 745.

45. George R. Thompson, and Dixie R. Harris, *The United States Army in World War II--The Technical Services--The Signal Corps: The Outcome (Mid-1943 Through 1945)* (Washington, D.C.: U.S. Government Printing Office, 1966), p. 108.

46. Ibid., p. 110.

47. U.S. 201st Field Press Censorship Organization, History of United States and Supreme Headquarters Allied Expeditionary Force Press Censorship in the European Theater of Operations, 1942-1945, p. 14.

48. Mott, p. 743.

49. Ibid., p. 205.

50. Ibid.

51. U.S. 201st Field Press Censorship Organization, History of United States and Supreme Headquarters Allied Expeditionary Force Press Censorship in the European Theater of Operations, 1942-1945, p. 119.

52. Ibid., pp. 116-18.

53. Susan D. Moeller, *Shooting War* (New York: Basic Books, 1989), p. 217.

54. Ibid.

55. Thompson and Harris, pp. 276, 299.

56. *Richard W. Steele, 'News of the 'Good War': World War II News Management.' Journalism Quarterly*, (62, No. 4 Winter 1985): 709.

57. Stein, p. 109.

58. Summers, p. 169; and Koop, *Weapon of Silence*, pp. 196-99.

59. Emery, p. 480.

60. William Manchester, *American Caesar: Douglas MacArthur 1880-1964* (New York: Dell, 1978), p. 416.

61. Koop, *Weapon of Silence*, p. 271.

62. Manchester, p. 482.

63. Lt. Col. Wallace B. Eberhard, U.S. Army, 'From Balloon Bombs to H-Bombs,' *Military Review*, (59, No. 2 February 1981): pp. 4-5.

64. Ibid, p. 4.

65. Koop, *Weapon of Silence*, pp. 202-4.

66. Ibid., p. 244.

67. Say, p. 140.

68. Ibid.

69. Ibid.

70. Ibid.

71. Ibid.

72. Mott, p. 763.

CHAPTER 5

U.S. WARTIME PRESS CENSORSHIP IN THE KOREAN WAR

When the Korean War began, no correspondents
accompanied U.S. forces deploying to Korea from Japan. As
the first correspondents trickled into Korea during June
1950, a policy of voluntary, self-censorship took effect.
Until U.S. ground forces arrived in July, however,
correspondents in Korea could not transmit their stories
out of the country. The stories that were filed were
shuttled to Japan without censorship and without any clear
voluntary censorship guidelines.[1] Even when U.S. ground
forces did arrive in Korea correspondents 'found that the
definition of security was so loose, even among Army
officers, that the correspondents could not adequately
judge for themselves.'[2]

The lack of guidance perplexed the correspondents
and infuriated the military. The guidance 'requested
nondisclosure of 'names and positions of units . . .
figures of friendly casualties . . . strength of
reinforcements . . . or any such information as may be of
aid and comfort to the enemy.''[3] In light of the

humiliating initial defeats suffered by the U.S. the

correspondents had plenty to write about:

> We couldn't stop them. They came at us from all
> sides. We fired till we ran out of ammo. . . . [It
> was] bad, sir. . . . The litter cases were
> abandoned.[4]

Since criticism of U.S. defeats did not violate the

vague voluntary censorship system:

> . . . aimed at preserving military secrecy . . .
> the correspondents wrote freely of "whipped and
> frightened GIs," of the panic, of the poor example
> set by many officers, of the lack of equipment--
> "you can't get a tank with a carbine"--of the
> general desperation, horror, and lack of purpose.[5]

The U.S. military did not accept this reporting as

fair and honest. "The army in Korea and at MacArthur's

headquarters in Tokyo accused the correspondents of being

traitors, of 'giving aid and comfort to the enemy.'" On 25

July 1950, the "army extended the voluntary code to rule

out any criticism of decisions made by United Nations

commanders in the field or of conduct by allied soldiers on

the battlefield."[6]

The voluntary censorship was kept alive by the

support of the United Nations commander:

> General Douglas MacArthur was adamant in his
> decision to avoid formal censorship by the use of a
> voluntary press code. "A true democratic free
> press," argued MacArthur, "will accept the
> challenge."[7]

MacArthur even continued his stand, temporarily, when

directed by the Joint Chiefs of Staff on 16 December 1950

to 'impose a news blackout and impound pertinent communications media . . .' to stop 'security leaks.'[8]

Not all his subordinates agreed. 'Correspondents did on occasion,' one of his staff wrote, 'reveal information through press and radio that was of value to the enemy.' The pressure of competition with other correspondents appeared to be the catalyst for these 'security violations.'[9]

Even Congress became concerned about 'breaches of security' and called on correspondents 'to stop disclosing troop movements in the Far East.'[10] The 'security violations' which concerned the United Nations forces in Korea included stories on the:

> . . . arrival of the U.S. Army 2nd Infantry Division in Korea at Pusan; arrival of the U.S. 1st Cavalry Division with an amphibious landing at Pohang; arrival of the initial British force; first landing of U.S. 1st Marine Division; loss of Major General William Dean; amphibious assault on the city of Inchon, port of Seoul (this was revealed ten hours before it actually happened); first entrance of the new U.S. Air Force Sabre jet (fighter) plane into combat.[11]

Correspondents chafed under both the vague censorship restrictions and the stigma of endangering allied forces. The restrictions, 'described by one correspondent as 'you write what you like and we'll shoot you if we don't like it,''[12] had their most famous violation in late 1950. Associated Press reporter Tom Lambert and United Press International reporter Peter Kalischer were 'accused of writing stories 'giving aid and

comfort to the enemy.'`[13]` The reporters were told during a
visit to the Far East Command headquarters in Tokyo that
they had been suspended from reporting the war. They:

> . . . would not be allowed to return to the Korean
> front. They had, the public information officer
> said, failed to observe `discretion and co-
> operation in the dispatch of their file` and had
> been guilty of disclosing information that would
> have `a bad moral and psychological effect` on the
> United Nations troops.`[14]`

Concerned that his correspondent had been
inaccurate in his reporting, the United Press International
Chief in Tokyo, Earnest Hoberecht, offered to print a
retraction. He withdrew the offer when he:

> . . . realized the main objection to the dispatches
> was that they `made the Army look bad,` he
> announced that United Press International `intended
> to print defeats when there were defeats` and
> `would be glad to report victories when there were
> victories.`[15]`

Lambert and Kalischer made representations to
MacArthur himself, who lifted the ban but took the
opportunity to remind all the correspondents that they had
`an important responsibility in the matter of psychological
warfare.`[16]`

The attitude of the United Nations command toward
voluntary censorship changed in December 1950. In
November, as the United Nations forces approached the Yalu
River and the North Korean border with China, Chinese
troops attacked. In the ensuing retreat, recriminations,
charges of cowardice and criticism between the allies
abounded. The truthful, harsh reports leaving Korea `were

101

not calculated to improve morale."[17]   Other reports in

December highlighted the South Korean government's

corruption, political arrests, and mass executions of men,

women, and children identified as communists.[18]

When faced with the mounting criticism and the

hard-pressed army's "need to conceal the identity, strength

and movement of friendly troops," the United Nations

command instituted involuntary press censorship in Korea

and Tokyo on December 20, 1950.[19]

The comments of the new chief censor upon assuming

his duties were:

> Our primary aim will be to prevent release of
> information that would endanger our troops or would
> be of value to the enemy. We will maintain a
> sympathetic attitude toward legitimate activities
> of all press representatives. We will not be
> arbitrary, unreasonable, or humorless, and we will
> have sound reason, though may not always be able to
> disclose it, for each action taken. We will
> proceed in the belief that the folks at home would
> rather get news a few hours late of a son who is
> living than news of a battle before it begins and
> then of a son who is dead.[20]

The new policy was welcomed by the correspondents,

who quickly learned the seriousness of the military

officers responsible for the program. On December 23rd,

the censorship showed its teeth after the death in an

automobile accident of the U.S. commander, General Walton

H. Walker. The reporter who broke the story, Peter Webb of

United Press International, had cleared it with the censor

in Tokyo,

. . . but when it appeared Eighth Army headquarters (in Korea) arrested Webb. It was eighteen hours before he was able to prove he had not violated censorship regulations, and he was then released.[21]

The World War II Office of Censorship Press Codes (Appendix 2) together with War Department supplements were pulled out of 'the depths of somebody's dusty file' and were 'adopted virtually *in toto*' by the U.S. censors.[22] The restrictions for Korea also included 'any discussion of allied air power' and 'the effect of enemy fire unless authorized.' Also restricted were 'any derogatory comments' about 'allied conduct of the war' or about allied troops or commanders.[23] After General Matthew Ridgeway arrived to replace Walker, he 'forbade further disclosure of our (the U.S.) order-of-battle (deployments and designation of troop units: corps, divisions, regiments, etc.).'[24]

In contrast to World War II, however, the methods of communication out of the theater were not controlled or censored, providing a ready method for any correspondent attempting to circumvent the censorship:

> No censorship of the mails had been imposed; commercial telegraph, radio, and cable facilities, all of which were available in some parts of Korea and all of Japan, were not monitored; nor were the Korea-Japan telephone circuits supervised.[25]

Restrictions did include the 'auditioning' of audio tapes. 'Offending passages were snipped out.'[26]

The pressure for a scoop sent some reporters scurrying for methods to circumvent the censorship. A

103

telephone code, called by the Army 'Twenty Questions,' was used by several newsmen to bypass censorship. Seemingly innocuous questions and answers disguised information which would not have passed censorship. Representative questions were: 'Are you coming over soon?' and 'When do you expect to come?' Their answers were: 'I think so,' and 'I'll try to leave in three or four days.' The disguised actual questions and answers were: 'Do you expect that we will surrender Seoul? Yes.' and 'When do you think we'll retreat from Seoul and go south to the Han? In the next three or four days.' This practice was 'broken up when the censors' learned of the practice and 'threatened to expel the guilty newsmen from Korea.'[27]

Another attempt to circumvent the censorship restrictions also involved correspondents 'scooping' their competitors. A correspondent sent his exclusive story on the U.N evacuation of Seoul during January 1951 to the Eighth Army headquarters censor. The censor held it. General Ridgway had:

> . . . requested that correspondents help conceal the withdrawal from the enemy by holding their news stories of the event until the tactical move was complete.[28]

Meanwhile, three other correspondents picked up the story and, ignoring General Ridgway's request, surreptitiously phoned it to their editors who 'broke the story.' 'One agency, because it had obeyed the rules, had been badly beaten, although it had started originally with a clear lead."[20]

During the confusing military situation of January 1951, the Far East Command delegated censorship responsibility from Tokyo to the Eighth Army headquarters in Korea for Army matters, and respectively to Headquarters, Naval Forces Far East and Headquarters, Far East Air Forces for naval and air matters.[30] After the military situation in Korea stabilized to some degree in March 1951, the Far East Command decreed that stories already censored by subordinate headquarters "should be 'reviewed' by censors in Tokyo. Thus was instituted the system of 'double censorship.'"[31]

During the period of "double censorship," censors at the Far East Command:

> . . . made no changes in the copy submitted, only necessary deletions. They did recommend revisions; and correspondents were always allowed to make necessary changes when deletions interrupted the continuity of their material.[32]

Though the censors tried through a "24-hour-a-day, 7-days-a-week" operation to minimize processing time, "the double check caused delays and also left (correspondents) in the dark as to what further cuts" had been made after the subordinate command censors sent the copy to Tokyo.[33]

The complaints resulted in the transfer of all censorship authority to Tokyo in June 1951, though the Far East Command maintained a censorship detachment in Korea.

During the remainder of the war, despite censorship
violations including the false report that General Ridgeway
suffered from "recurrent heart attacks"[34] and the
publication of sensitive order of battle information in
Newsweek magazine,[35] the Far East Command censors
"attempted to release the maximum of information."[36]

Simultaneously, charges against the Far East
Command of "news suppression" were made by correspondents
for incidents including orders that prohibited "returning
(allied) prisoners from revealing their experiences in
Communist camps"[37] and for the blackout of reports on
rioting North Korean prisoners in the Koje-do prisoner-of-
war camp.[38] Despite these charges and the fact that:

> . . . the inherently competitive nature of
> reporting and security requirements are natural
> enemies, most correspondents, especially seasoned
> ones, and the editors involved in covering the
> Korean conflict met the demands of censorship
> fairly . . . And (in general) there were few
> protests by newsmen over censorship.[39]

Conclusions on Korean War Censorship

Though wartime press censorship by the U.S. in the
Korean War became involuntary, compliance was completely
voluntary. Correspondents were allowed unrestricted access
to available commercial (and in some cases military)
communications circuits. In general, the military
leadership initially wanted voluntary censorship and only
accepted mandatory censorship reluctantly, while the
preponderance of correspondents wanted involuntary

censorship from the outset to remove the onus from them of
violating military security to ensure a scoop.

CHAPTER 5 ENDNOTES

1. Marguerite Higgins, *War in Korea-The Report of A Woman Combat Correspondent* (Garden City, N.Y.: Doubleday, 1951), pp. 27-31.

2. Peter Braestrop, *Battle Lines* (New York: Priority Press Publications, 1985), p. 51.

3. Susan D. Moeller, *Shooting War* (New York: Basic Books, 1989), p. 279.

4. Higgins, p. 69.

5. Phillip Knightley, *The First Casualty* (New York: Harcourt, Brace, Jovanovich, 1976), p. 337.

6. Ibid.

7. Moeller, p. 279.

8. Ibid., p. 300.

9. Lieutenant Colonel Melvin B. Voorhees, U.S. Army, *Korean Tales* (New York: Simon and Schuster, 1952), p. 104.

10. Braestrup, p. 52.

11. Voorhees, p. 104.

12. Knightley, p. 337.

13. Higgins, p. 95.

14. Knightley, p. 337.

15. Colonel Thomas J. Cleary, Jr., U.S. Army, 'Aid and Comfort to the Enemy,' *Military Review*, (48, No. 8, August 1988): 54.

16. Knightley, p. 337.

17. Ibid., p. 343.

18. Ibid.

19. Braestrup, p. 53.

20. Voorhees, p. 102.

21. Knightley, p. 345.

22. Voorhees, p. 111.

23. Knightley, pp. 345-46.

24. Voorhees, p. 105.

25. Braestrup, p. 57.

26. Ibid., p. 56.

27. Voorhees, pp. 106-7.

28. Braestrup, p. 55.

29. Voorhees, pp. 109-10.

30. Braestrup, p. 56.

31. Voorhees, p. 112.

32. Ibid.

33. Ibid., pp. 56-57.

34. Braestrup, p. 58.

35. Voorhees, pp. 113-14; and Braestrup, pp. 58-59.

36. Braestrup, p. 60.

37. Knightley, p. 351.

38. Braestrup, p. 59, and Robert Leckie, *The Wars of America* (New York: Harper and Row, 1981), pp. 921-22.

39. Braestrup, p. 60.

CHAPTER 6

THE DEBATE OVER PRESS CENSORSHIP IN THE VIETNAM WAR

In January 1965, President Lyndon Johnson
authorized U.S. forces in Southeast Asia to conduct a
'heavy attack on an important bridge in Laos.' When Radio
Hanoi and Radio Peking protested the attack, charging the
U.S. with escalating its involvement in the war, State and
Defense department spokesmen waffled. In the absence of a
U.S. denial of the communist accusations, correspondents in
Saigon reported the attacks as a deepening of the U.S.
involvement in the war.[1]

The characterization of the attack as a further
commitment of U.S. forces in the region was inimical to the
U.S. administration's desires. 'Johnson wanted to avoid
appearing to escalate the war, but the press continued to
emphasize the widening nature of American involvement.'[2]

President Johnson's displeasure with the news
stories coming from Saigon was felt by General William C.
Westmoreland, the commander of the U.S. Military Assistance

Command, Vietnam (MACV). During a visit to Saigon by U.S.

Senator Monroney, Johnson's views were made known:

> Convinced that Monroney was Johnson's personal
> emissary, General Westmoreland had few doubts about
> the senator's meaning: the president was becoming
> increasingly concerned about the U.S. mission's
> failure to keep the Saigon correspondents under
> control.[3]

When the U.S. began stepped-up attacks against

North Vietnam in February 1965, the administration's

displeasure with press criticism and with the publication

of 'potentially damaging information' increased. U.S.

forces in Southeast Asia were forced by the administration

to decide whether to implement drastic measures, including

censorship, to restrict correspondents reporting the war.

As a stopgap measure, Barry Zorthian, the public affairs

officer of the U.S. Mission to Saigon, distributed a

memorandum to Saigon-based correspondents which asked their

voluntary cooperation in refraining from publishing

information which would 'help the enemy,' particularly

details of ongoing air attacks. Simultaneously, Zorthian

sought firm administration direction for future press

restrictions.[4]

Correspondents' access to operational information

in 'South Vietnam was so open and news sources so abundant'

that there was little that could be done to restrict the

flow of 'sensitive' information from Southeast Asia.

Westmoreland supported Zorthian's effort to obtain firm

administration information policy direction. In a February

1965 message to the Chairman of the Joint Chiefs of Staff

he said:

> Since the rules of the game are changing rapidly,
> it seems to me that we should consider [censorship]
> arrangements similar to those exercised in the
> Korean conflict. This would involve providing for
> accredited war correspondents (we may want to give
> them another name) and censorship in some form.[5]

Westmoreland wrote of his thoughts on invoking

censorship in his autobiography. His misgivings were

representative of arguments against establishing formal

censorship during the war:

> As large numbers of American ground troops were
> committed, I seriously considered recommending
> press censorship. Yet I saw many obstacles. How,
> for example, to prevent reporters, including many
> from countries other than the United States, from
> filing their stories from some other country, as
> enterprising newsmen did during the fighting
> against the Moros in the Philippines at the turn of
> the century? Such cities as Bangkok, Manila,
> Singapore and Hong Kong were readily accessible.
> As for television, the very mechanics of censoring
> it was forbidding to contemplate, particularly
> since it would have had to be administered by the
> sovereign power, South Vietnam, whose ability to do
> it was questionable.[6]

In March 1965 the idea of invoking censorship

received serious consideration by the administration after:

> Saigon correspondents made a series of revelations
> that threatened both operational security and
> American relations with the South Vietnamese. The
> breach occurred following a decision by President
> Johnson on 26 February to send two battalions of
> U.S. Marines to protect Da Nang Air Base . . .
> vital to attacks against North Vietnam. . . .
>   In compliance with South Vietnamese wishes, the
> State and Defense Departments ordered the U.S.
> mission in Saigon to prevent premature disclosure
> of the landing. Reporters at Da Nang could
> nevertheless see that the base was preparing for
> the arrival of American troops. On 2 March they

112

filed dispatches to that effect. . . . [T]he
revelation . . . startled official Washington.[7]

These reports, combined with increased reporting of
the air campaign against North Vietnam and Laos, *Rolling
Thunder*, were at first attributed by the administration to
news leaks. In March 1965, however, Westmoreland told
Secretary of Defense McNamara that the real source of the
stories, open access of newsmen to information in South
Vietnam, required that censorship policy "must be modified
in view of the changed nature of (U.S.) military
activities."[8]

The director of the U.S. Information Agency, Carl
Rowan, cabled the State Department from Saigon during a
March 1965 visit that censorship must be considered in
light of the reporting of operational information. He
expressed reservations about formal censorship in Vietnam
and said:

> . . . correspondents were competing strenuously for
> what news there was and that more irresponsible
> revelations were bound to result. Control was
> impossible under non-wartime conditions, but some
> arrangement to reduce current difficulties seemed
> imperative. At the very least, contingency
> planning should begin for the "stringent measures"
> [censorship] that would become necessary if the war
> escalated much further.[9]

During a conference in Hawaii later in March 1965,
information representatives of "all U.S. government
agencies concerned with the war in South Vietnam . . .
rejected any form of field press censorship, opting for the
system of voluntary cooperation" which had been in effect

since February. The attendees noted that the support of the American people necessary to win the war was "likely to waver if any significant number of our people believe . . . they are being misled."[10]

The rejection of censorship by the conference attendees was based on several factors:

> Censorship would require the legal underpinnings of a declaration of war as well as an enormous logistical and administrative effort. The censors would need jurisdiction over all communications and transportation facilities connecting South Vietnam with the rest of the world and parallel authority over civilian mail. That would necessitate a large number of multilingual military personnel to do the censoring and expanded, U.S.-controlled teletype and radio circuits in South Vietnam to move the censored material. Even if the United States could meet those conditions, the South Vietnamese remained an unknown quantity. Since they were responsible for their own internal affairs, they would necessarily play an important part in any censorship program. Yet lacking a concept of American-style freedom of the press, they would undoubtedly exercise their prerogatives with a heavy hand. In any case, many Saigon correspondents were foreigners beyond the reach of American military regulations and likely to resist any attempt to bring them under control.[11]

The final conference report's recommendations, approved and adopted in April 1965, provided for voluntary cooperation and not censorship. In return for agreeing to abide by ground rules, correspondents received accreditation which authorized them access to the theater of operations and combat areas, military transportation around South Vietnam, access to military messing and billeting, use of communications facilities and courier services, recreational facilities outside Saigon, and

114

emergency medical care. In many cases accreditation
authorized correspondents to purchase US military field
clothing, and to use military exchanges and
commissaries.[12]

Possibly of more importance to correspondents,
accreditation authorized them 'access to important
briefings and interviews' and also to 'gain entry to
candid, sometimes classified information.'[13] Those who
refused to agree to the rules would be denied these
privileges.[14]

The ground rules adopted in 1965 remained in effect
throughout the war with only minor revisions. The October
1966 version is contained in Appendix 3.

The appearance in the U.S. media later in April
1965 of stories on the growing U.S. air and land
involvement in South Vietnam and stories criticizing the
use of tear gas infuriated President Johnson and caused
formal censorship to be reconsidered. General Wheeler, the
JCS Chairman, complained to Westmoreland that 'the
situation in the U.S. is exacerbated and pressures upon
highest authority increased by press coverage' of these
issues. He further asked Westmoreland to recommend a
solution and said, 'It may well be that nothing short of
press censorship will serve this end.'[15]

The MACV response reiterated that 'practical
considerations' made censorship impossible. Westmoreland's

superior, Admiral U.S.G. Sharp, Commander-in-Chief, Pacific
Command, agreed:

> In view of the increasing tempo of air strikes and
> proposed deployments in South Vietnam, I expect
> press coverage to move into an even higher key. As
> we escalate, so will reporting of the press. I
> doubt that even with field press censorship this
> could be avoided, and it is quite likely that
> censorship would have an inflammatory effect.[16]

In a briefing in Washington in February 1968,
former Secretary of State Dean Rusk made clear the position
of the Johnson administration on censorship, 'Unless we are
in a formal state of war, with censorship here, there is no
point in having censorship (in Vietnam). . . . Here is
where most leaks come.'[17]

Despite these strong positions against censorship,
the administration brought up the issue again after the new
MACV ground rules were violated in August 1965 by CBS News
reporter Morely Safer. Safer had infuriated both the
administration and MACV by preparing a news report showing
U.S. Marines torching a Vietnamese village with Zippo
cigarette lighters. Later in the month he reported, in
violation of MACV ground rules, that 'U.S. airborne troops
were on the move to Pleiku and might relieve a besieged
Special Forces camp.'[18]

Assistant Secretary of Defense for Public Affairs
Arthur Sylvester wrote to CBS News president Fred Friendly
and asked that Safer be recalled. He argued that Safer, a

Canadian, should be replaced by an American who would be

'more sensitive to the situation.' Friendly disagreed:

> The suggestion that an American might be more
> sensitive to the situation than a Canadian was
> tantamount to saying that an American would be
> 'more 'sympathetic'' to the official line.[19]

Friendly completely rejected Sylvester's arguments

for Safer's recall in a statement which is representative

of press arguments against censorship in Vietnam:

> The essence of our dispute is quite simple. You
> don't want anything you consider damaging to our
> morale or our world-wide image reported. We don't
> want to violate purely *military* security with
> reports which could endanger the life of a single
> soldier but, by the same token, we must insist upon
> our right to report what is actually happening
> despite the political consequences.[20]

Sylvester was so concerned after this violation

that he ordered the drafting of a censorship plan.[21]

Though the plan finally developed was 'so ponderous that it

could never become a serious alternative to the voluntary

guidelines already in effect,' its completion ended 'all

(administration) consideration of field press censorship in

South Vietnam.'[22]

Correspondents in Saigon did not give up on the

idea. In 1968, 'a group of Saigon bureau chiefs' met with

Major General Winant Sidle, then chief of information for

MACV:

> . . . and asked that I take steps to institute
> field press censorship. Their point was that the
> press should not have to censor itself; the
> government should do it. The group backed off when
> it realized that South Vietnam, as the sovereign
> nation, might well also have censorship rights

117

should the United States initiate field press censorship.[23]

Censorship of Photographs and Film

The Department of Defense and MACV developed firm voluntary press restrictions in the summer of 1965, but did not address specific guidelines on news photography and television and movie film. The problem was new to the Vietnam conflict. The speed with which photographs and film could be prepared and transported by jet or electronic means to the U.S. made it possible that the first knowledge a soldier's family had of his death or injury in combat might be seeing the event on the evening news or in a daily newspaper. This occurred in April 1967 when the parents of a soldier serving in Vietnam saw their son on the evening news after he had been wounded by a booby trap. The family was notified by the Army the next day.[24] Television was of particular concern to the government and the armed forces in:

> . . . that sound-on-sound film pictures of dying Americans would have a strong adverse emotional impact on families with husbands and sons serving in the war.[25]

Censorship of television film was considered, but for MACV to censor television without censoring print or photographic news material would have had 'serious consequences for official credibility.' The point proved moot in that television film shot in South Vietnam was

118

normally developed outside the country, eliminating the opportunity for MACV to review it.[26]

Throughout the war, photographs were sent to the U.S. using telegraphic wire photo services from Saigon to relay stations in Tokyo or San Francisco.[27] Television film was normally carried by hand to the networks on scheduled passenger flights to the U.S. One account of the process spoke of correspondents typically running to the airport to catch outgoing planes, 'vaulting the turnstile . . . (running) right out to the airplane and right up the steps as they were about to withdraw the ladder and close the door and (handing the film) to a passenger or stewardess.'[28]

After much debate, the Department of Defense and MACV formally rejected photographic and film censorship in April 1966. Voluntary guidelines were presented to television and film executives in the U.S. to 'emphasize the need for discrimination when selecting film footage for broadcast.'[29] The guidelines MACV presented to correspondents in Saigon were more firm, and said 'if complaints about film footage of the dead and wounded arose, commanders in the field would undoubtedly deny cameramen the right to accompany troops into combat.'[30]

The guidelines read in part:

The most personally sensitive information in any war is that pertaining to casualties . . . In the war in Vietnam complete reliance has been placed on news media representatives. There has been no

119

effort to impose restrictions on movement of audio-
visual correspondents in the field or to require
in-country processing, review and editing of audio-
visual material produced by accredited
correspondents. We hope to preserve these freedoms
and ask that correspondents cooperate by--
    a. Not taking close-up pictures of casualties
that show faces or anything else that will identify
the individual.
    b. Not interviewing or recording the voices of
casualties until a medical officer determines that
the man is physically and mentally able, and the
individual gives permission.[31]

The voluntary guidelines worked. Dead and wounded

Americans rarely appeared on television news. Despite

television film crews accompanying U.S. troops daily into

combat, few battle scenes were broadcast. Part of the

explanation for the absence of battle scenes is that battle

was not an everyday event in Vietnam. Firefights were

often few and far between. Another factor is that the

television networks themselves expressed concern `about

offending the families of killed or wounded soldiers if

coverage was too graphic.`[32] In a contemporary CBS-TV

directive the guidelines were clear:

Producers and editors must exercise great caution
before permitting pictures of casualties to be
shown. This also applies to pictures of soldiers
in a state of shock. Obviously, good taste and
consideration for families of the deceased, wounded
or shocked takes precedence. Shots can be selected
that are not grisly, the purpose being not to avoid
showing the ugly side of war, but rather of
avoiding offending families of war victims.[33]

One study showed that for the nearly 200,000

casualties suffered by U.S. forces from August 1965 to

August 1970 (of a total of over 210,000 U.S. casualties for

the entire conflict)[34] only 76 out of 2,300 television news reports studied during the period depicted 'heavy fighting--soldiers in combat, incoming artillery, dead and wounded on the ground.'[35] A second study showed that during 167 televised reports covering the vigorously reported *Tet Offensive* in 1968, 'only 16 had more than one video shot of the dead or wounded.'[36] A third study showed that of 'Vietnam-related television news stories filmed from 1968 to 1973 . . . only 2 percent showed any dead or wounded.'[37]

An Assessment of the Censorship Decision

Though considered, no serious attempt to invoke U.S. wartime press censorship occurred during the Vietnam War. Columnist Drew Middleton, a correspondent in several wars including Vietnam, argued from a decidedly minority viewpoint that censorship should have been established:

> . . . we fought the war without military censorship. The American officers of World War II, when censorship was in effect, had little to complain about in the conduct of the accredited war correspondents. That was largely because commanders could take reporters into their confidence in regard to what was really going on, knowing the information would not land in the papers the next day and become available to the enemy. This relationship, in a war in which Americans were solidly united, bore fruit in knowledgeable and authoritative reporting on the strategic and tactical aspects of the campaigns in Europe and the Pacific. No such relationship was possible in an engagement that the Johnson administration chose to fight without invoking the rules of all-out military effort, either in the economy or on the home front or in its information policies.[38]

Middleton also blamed both the negative attitudes of military officers toward the press and the critical tone of reporting the war on the lack of censorship. Middleton said both he and many military officers in Vietnam felt censorship may have prevented the media from "being against us." He also said in an interview, "There were a lot of (military) people only too quick to blame the media for selling them out . . . for writing (only) the bad news."[39]

In a letter to author Phillip Knightley, he argued that correspondents couldn't get the true picture because military officers not protected by censorship were unwilling to talk to reporters:

> On three trips to Vietnam, I found generals and everyone else far more wary of talking to reporters precisely because there was no censorship. Their usual line with a difficult or sensitive question was "You must ask the public relations people about that." The latter, usually of low rank, clammed up, and the reporter and the public got less.[40]

Even before the decision not to impose censorship was made, *Los Angeles Times* reporter Jack Foisie wrote in support of censorship, "Racehorses need a starting gate for an equal start, and so do correspondents."[41] Foisie's own later experience demonstrated his frustration with the competition for stories the lack of censorship caused. His accreditation was suspended for 30 days for reporting a U.S. Marine amphibious landing in January 1966 "prior to official release of the information."[42]

Howard K. Smith, an ABC News correspondent during Vietnam, said after the war,

> I think there had to be military censorship in Vietnam . . . We've had it in every war this century. Vietnam is the only one we didn't have it and I think we needed it. Political censorship you can't have. I believe firmly there should have been a military censorship.[43]

Most authors on the subject disagree with these views. During the war, "journalists in Vietnam were free to go where they pleased and report what they wished," political science and communications professor Daniel Hallin wrote, "No journalist I interviewed ever told me that military restrictions had any impact on coverage."[44]

Former *Detroit Free Press* Vietnam correspondent Robert L. Pisor went to the opposite end of the spectrum from Middleton when he said "field press censorship is impossible." He added:

> Our tradition from the very beginning--written into our Constitution, written into our national fiber-- is the belief we are a stronger democracy because people know more about what's going on. . . . That is so thoroughly a part of our fiber that there would be reporters who would work around a censorship rule.[45]

George Esper, one of the Associated Press's Saigon bureau chief during the war, also opposed censorship. He called the imposition of censorship during war "self defeating" and said it would have upset the "principles of a democratic free press" and would result in the fall of any democracy.[46]

Furthermore, the voluntary restrictions worked.
Zorthian wrote:

> Vietnam was probably the first war fought without
> censorship, on center stage, in the full glare of
> the floodlights. When the press was asked in
> Vietnam to respect legitimate rules of protection
> of tactical military security, it did. There were
> 4,000 press accreditations in Vietnam while I was
> there [1964-70], and over a period of four and one-
> half years only five correspondents had their
> credentials lifted for violating military security.
> If our benchmark had been violation of political
> security, violating all the information that the
> Government tried or would have liked to have kept
> secure, then most of the press would have had their
> credentials lifted.[47]

Conclusions on Censorship in the Vietnam War

The decision not to impose censorship in Vietnam
remains controversial today. The decision not to invoke it
was based more on political considerations than on concerns
about the difficulty of administering the program. Though
the administration professed concern at the impossibility
of preventing reporters from filing their stories outside
Vietnam or at the logistical difficulty of censoring modern
communications and television, these problems were only
slightly different from those faced by censors in previous
wars. Of greater concern was the political unpopularity of
the war at home and the unpalatable concept of censorship
administered in cooperation with the South Vietnamese. The
most significant factor in the decision not to impose
censorship in Vietnam was that the international news media
were beyond the reach of American military control and were

likely to resist or ignore any attempt to bring them under control.

CHAPTER 6 ENDNOTES

1. William M. Hammond, *Public Affairs: The Military and the Media* (Washington, D.C.: U.S. Government Printing Office, 1988) pp. 133-34.

2. Ibid., p. 133.

3. Ibid., pp. 134-35

4. Ibid., pp. 137-38.

5. Ibid., p. 138.

6. General William C. Westmoreland, U.S. Army, *A Soldier Reports* (New York: Dell, 1980), p. 359.

7. Hammond, pp. 138-39.

8. Ibid., p. 139.

9. Ibid., p. 140.

10. Ibid., pp. 143-45.

11. Ibid., pp. 144-45.

12. U.S. Military Assistance Command, Vietnam, *Public Information Policies and Procedures (Military Assistance Command-Vietnam Directive 360-1)*, Saigon, 1967, pp. 12-14.

13. Hammond, p. 145.

14. "News Media Warned on Censorship Rules," *The Washington Post*, 13 August 1965, p. A9.

15. Hammond, p. 160.

16. Ibid.

17. Daniel C. Hallin, *The Uncensored War* (New York: Oxford University Press, 1986), p. 213.

18. Hammond, pp. 188-90.

19. Ibid., p. 191.

20. Ibid.

21. Ibid., p. 193.

22. Ibid., p. 195.

23. Maj. Gen. Winant Sidle, USA Ret 'The Public's Right to Know,' *Proceedings*, (111/7/989, July 1985): 43.

24. 'Parents See G.I. Son Wounded on TV,' *The New York Times*, 12 May 1967, p. 3.

25. Hammond, p. 237.

26. Ibid.

27. Moeller, p. 362.

28. Ibid., p. 361.

29. Hammond, p. 238.

30. Ibid., pp. 237-38.

31. Moeller, p. 365.

32. Hallin, p. 130.

33. Ibid.

34. U.S. Department of Defense, 'Defense 89 Almanac,' Washington, D.C., September-October 1989, p. 47.

35. Hammond, p. 238.

36. Hallin, p. 130.

37. Braestrup, p. 69.

38. Drew Middleton, 'Vietnam and the Military Mind,' *The New York Times Magazine*, 10 January 1982, p. 34.

39. Lt. Col. Gerald. W. Sharpe, U.S. Army, 'Army/Media Conflict: Origins, Development and Recommendations,' Unpublished student thesis, U.S. Army War College, Carlisle Barracks, Pa., 1986, p. 140.

40. Knightley, p. 423.

41. Jack Foisie, 'My Third War,' *Army* (15, No. 15 October 1965): 34.

42. 'U.S. Reporter in Vietnam is Suspended for a Month.' *The New York Times*, 1 February 1966, p. 14.

43. U.S. Department of Defense, Defense Information School, *Vietnam 10 Years Later* (Fort Benjamin Harrison, Ind.: U.S. Government Printing Office, 1984), p. 61.

44. Hallin, pp. 129, 233.

45. U.S. Department of Defense, Defense Information School, *Vietnam 10 Years Later* (Fort Benjamin Harrison, Ind.: U.S. Government Printing Office, 1984), p. 73.

46. Ibid., pp. 49-51.

47. Barry Zorthian, "The Role of the Communications Media in a Democratic Society," *Naval War College Review*, (24, No. 6, February 1972): 6.

CHAPTER 7

U.S. WARTIME PRESS CENSORSHIP TODAY

The debate over U.S. Wartime Press Censorship ended
in 1987 with the elimination of the Wartime Information
Security Program (Appendix 4) and its armed forces
counterpart, Field Press Censorship (Appendix 5).[1]

The legacies of Grenada and Vietnam were the
primary cause of the elimination. The controversial
exclusion of reporters from the U.S. invasion of Grenada in
1983, Operation *Urgent Fury*, was not accompanied by serious
consideration of the imposition of censorship. The U.S.
forces did not accredit correspondents until a pool of
reporters was organized on Barbados and transported to
Grenada on the third day of the operation.[2] Though
correspondents, including four Americans, arrived on
Grenada the morning of the invasion they were unable to
communicate with the outside world and had little contact
with U.S. forces until shortly before the U.S.-accredited
press pool arrived.[3]

Therefore, the impetus to impose censorship during
Urgent Fury was reduced by the absence of any

correspondents creating news material to censor until combat had ended. In fact, procedures to ask the National Command Authority to impose field press censorship were not part of planning procedures then in force.⁴

As a result of the controversial exclusion of correspondents from Grenada, the Department of Defense developed the National Media Pool to ensure media access to future military operations. The first operational use of the pool was a deployment to the Persian Gulf in July 1987 to cover U.S. escort operations of merchant shipping. The pool's news products were subject to a "security review" by public affairs officers before release. The materials prepared by the pool "were reviewed for security and changes were recommended, if warranted." The products, audio, video, still photographs, and print, were dispatched from U.S. Navy ships in the Gulf by "all available means." Though some concern was expressed about "censorship of pool products," the security review process was recognized as necessary to prevent the "release of operational information (which) puts U.S. lives at risk." The almost complete dependence of the pool members on military communications facilities ensured compliance, and the pool members reluctantly came to accept the restrictions.⁵

The elimination of the Wartime Information Security Program and Field Press Censorship in 1987 also removed any consideration of censorship from U.S. planning for operations in Panama in December 1989, Operation *Just Cause.*⁵ However, the national media pool which deployed to Panama did use the same vestige of censorship used in the Persian Gulf. Print journalists serving with the media pool were subject to a 'security review' of their copy by military public affairs officers prior to its transmission by military communications channels to Washington. The review was usually an informal check of a print correspondent's copy prior to dispatch.⁷

The review requirement proved surprisingly uncontroversial despite the fact that it did not apply to TV reporters accompanying the pool or to any of the correspondents already in Panama.⁸ Pool broadcast correspondents and all non-pool correspondents from any media in Panama were allowed to file their stories over civilian communications channels without being subject to security review. The only restriction for pool broadcast correspondents was supervision by a military escort officer.⁹

The pace of the reporting caused at least two print correspondents accompanying the pool to bypass the security review process. 'Bob Kearns of Reuters and Steven Komarow of the Associated Press . . . dictated (reports) by phone directly to their wire services.'¹⁰

The Effects of Technology

Improvements in communications and video technology during the 1980's have given correspondents the capability to transmit news instantly via satellite throughout the world using equipment carried by one man.[11] To explain the problems this capability causes any attempt to restrict the flow of information from a theater of war, a survey of current communications technology available to correspondents is necessary.

Two types of communications are of interest to correspondents attempting to transmit news materials from a theater of war: surface and radio. The surface communications transmission technologies available in the U.S. and in much of the world are mainly telephone-type audio or data lines and cable television lines. They take the form of twisted wire, coaxial cable, or optical fibers. These three technologies between them have provided decades of reliable, inexpensive audio and telegraphic communications services, including transoceanic submarine cable, to and from the world's major cities. In more recent years, these technologies have spread to much of the Third World. The bottom line on surface communications technology is that in almost any city on earth, the proliferation of international telephone and telegraph facilities give correspondents a means to transmit news stories by voice to the U.S. quickly and reliably. Most worldwide surface communications service is capable of transmitting audio and data transmissions but is unable to transmit video transmissions. Surface communications circuits capable of carrying video transmissions are limited for the most part to urban areas.[12]

The second communications technology, radio, consists of microwave transmission, cellular radio, and communications satellites, and is intertwined with surface communications technology. This means that in most industrialized nations, and in a significant part of the Third World, microwave high frequency radio transmissions are used to carry long-haul audio, data, and video transmissions, including most telephone traffic. Surface and radio communications are interdependent. Satellite communications relays handle most transoceanic telephone and telegraph traffic, and much domestic traffic in many countries. Cellular radio offers audio and data communications capability throughout the urban areas of most industrialized nations by using land-based receivers and transmitters. Cellular radio also offers limited satellite links which can give audio and data communications capability throughout the world.[13]

Though microwave transmissions, cellular radio and surface communications technology are the means correspondents in urban areas transmit news materials to their editors or stations, the technology which most affects the coverage of military operations in theaters of war is satellite communications. Using man-portable satellite earth stations, a correspondent can transmit audio, data, photos, or in some cases, pre-recorded video images to thousands of other earth stations throughout the world.[14] The only regions of the earth not readily accessible to most satellite communications are the polar regions.[15]

Of more significance to correspondents than portable earth stations are the fixed satellite earth stations. Currently, correspondents prefer that radio, photographic and print materials prepared in isolated areas be transmitted over the nearest telephone or telegraph links to editors or to broadcast networks and stations. In most cases, however, video materials of news events in isolated areas or of news events of interest outside a geographic region originate from hand-carried videotape or microwave transmission brought to a fixed-site earth station for relay. Currently, equipment necessary to transmit live video images is not man-portable. A fixed-site earth station is required.[16]

However, this situation is changing. When the National Media Pool travelled to Panama in December 1989, it arrived with a 'portable' satellite earth station capable of transmitting live video images. This NBC-TV equipment, though 'portable,' was bulky and weighed more than 2,000 lbs. After being flown to Panama on a U.S. Air

Force transport, it was used to file news reports directly to the U.S. under the supervision of a military escort officer.[17]

Most analysts agree that of the areas where the U.S. is likely to become engaged in combat the most likely is in a Third World country. Correspondent access to fixed-site satellite earth stations is surprisingly high in the Third World. Third World countries rely heavily on satellite communications even for routine domestic telephone use, resulting in a disproportionate proliferation of earth stations.[18] For example, during the Panama operation, correspondents were able to transport or transmit their video materials to earth stations in Panama and other Central American countries, and were able to use international telephone lines to transmit photographs and news stories to the U.S.[19]

The problem communications technology brings to an attempt to restrict the flow of news material from a theater of war is simple. Correspondents today cannot be prevented from communicating with the outside world unless they are separated from their communications equipment or are denied access to telephone or other communications means. With the proliferation of communications means and the easy access of satellite communications, attempts to prevent the transmission of or conduct 'security review' of news products may be impossible in all but the most isolated areas, and then only of the members of the national media pool.

The Debate Over U.S. Wartime Press Censorship

The U.S. media and the U.S. government have historically had competing purposes. The media views itself as a vigorous watchdog while the government views itself as defending national survival.

The U.S. armed forces and government want to prevent enemy access to information which could be used to jeopardize the lives of Americans or their allies. In addition, the armed forces and the government want to reduce or eliminate any criticism of their policies which may lower morale or damage the image of the U.S. in the eyes of the world. The government is also conscious of how fragile Congressional and public support becomes for use of the U.S. armed forces when Americans begun to die in combat.

The U.S. media on the other hand believe the U.S. is a strong democracy only because the American people know what is going on in America and the world. Though the news media acknowledge the necessity of protecting information which could endanger our servicemen and women, it insists upon the right to report what is happening regardless of any political consequences.

In American history, the conduct of wartime press censorship by the U.S. armed forces has consistently illuminated the competition between a nation at war and a free press. Particularly at the beginning of our conflicts, the focus of the media and the government are different.

Immediately before and during the initial stages of any of our conflicts, the news media were under tremendous pressure to provide information to the American people. The source of this pressure was not only a desire to inform but also a keen desire to "scoop" the competition and management concerns for advertising sales. This pressure to produce was not lessened but heightened by reverses or defeats.

On the other hand, immediately before and during the initial stages of any of our conflicts, the U.S. armed forces focused more on winning than on providing information to the news media. When the U.S. was winning, there was little need to impose censorship. Even when the outcome of a conflict was in doubt, if the tone of reporting was positive the impetus to censor was reduced. Indeed, if the news media "got on the team" there was little need to censor.

However, when the U.S. was losing or if the news med? reported reverses or became critical of the conduct of the war, the government was more likely to impose harsh censorship. Our military history is replete with examples. From Bull Run in the Civil War, to Pearl Harbor and the

Ardennes in World War II, to the Chinese intervention in Korea, censorship immediately clamped the lid on the reporting of both reverses and criticism.

This study has identified several arguments present in the debate over implementation of wartime press censorship in all major U.S. conflicts. Factors opposing and supporting censorship follow.

In opposition to censorship, the first argument was that censorship was not effective. Spies, it was argued, could provide an enemy with any information kept out of the news media. In addition, this argument submits that censorship was ineffective because it was inconsistent. Information kept from the news media by any particular censor in a theater of war was often either passed by other censors or made available to the media in areas not subject to censorship by news 'leaks.' In addition, it was argued as early as the Mexican War that the military could not consistently control communications from a theater of war. Censorship could easily be circumvented.

The second argument in opposition to censorship was that inconsistent enforcement ruined any censorship effort. Repeatedly in our history, it was argued, political or personal favoritism resulted in the censorship of some correspondents' copy while passing others.

A third argument was that censorship in most of our conflicts did not apply to anyone but correspondents.

Civilians who were not correspondents and soldiers in the field could often write letters home containing information that would have been censored in a news story.

A fourth argument was that censorship was used to shield the vanity of U.S. generals or to hide the corruption of military and civilian leadership. Censorship was used, it was argued, to hide from the American people defective weapons or faulty tactics, atrocities, and unhealthy living conditions of U.S. soldiers. This misuse of censorship, it was argued, delayed any outcry for corrective action.

A fifth argument was that the true nature of our allies was often hidden by censorship. The corruption, incompetence, political arrests, and mass executions of the Nationalist Chinese and the Soviets in World War II and the South Koreans during the Korean War, it was argued, were effectively hidden from the American people.

Another argument was that censorship was not necessary. History is replete with examples, it was argued, that correspondents with access to information, including the Normandy invasion and the development of the A-bomb, recognized the need to maintain secrecy. During our conflicts with and without censorship, it was also argued, the method of enforcing voluntary or involuntary restrictions, the "stick" of lifting a correspondent's accreditation to accompany U.S. forces, was rarely used.

The final argument against censorship was that it violated traditional American press freedom. In order to support any war effort, it was argued, the American people have a right to know.

On the other hand, in support of censorship, several arguments were presented. The first argument is that the requirement for security is paramount. That is, a nation can survive without a free press but it cannot survive without maintaining security. Our history is full of examples, it was argued, of U.S. opponents from Antonio Lopez de Santa Anna and Robert E. Lee to Manuel Noriega using the U.S. news media as a source of information on the plans and movements of the U.S. armed forces.

A second argument in support of censorship was that with the routine access of correspondents in theaters of war to classified information, only censorship could protect security. From the deployment of the ironclad *Monitor* in the Civil War, to the breaking of the Japanese naval codes and the development of radar in World War II, to the arrival of the first F-86 *Sabre* fighter jets in Korea, it was argued, only censorship could protect security.

A third argument for censorship was that it enables any military officer or civilian official to be completely open with the news media, knowing they would be protected from compromising classified information by the censor's review. On the other hand, a lack of censorship, it was argued, aggravated an already adversarial relationship and made U.S. leaders more reluctant to discuss troo- dispositions and plans and caused the news media and hence the American people to know less than they would have known under censorship.

A final argument was that censorship eliminates any need for competition between the news media for 'scoops.' All correspondents, it was argued, had an equal start with censorship.

In the end, America's traditional press freedom has outweighed any possible benefits offered by wartime press censorship. The capability and the national will to impose censorship are gone. Based on World War II and Korean War experience, for censorship to be effective, literally thousands of multi-lingual, mature, well-trained, carefully briefed military officers will be needed to implement any wartime press censorship system. There is no such pool of officers and to create such a pool after war is declared would be difficult. The U.S. would also need to have an effective method of controlling communications from the theater of war. This is also unlikely. Technological improvement, governmental reluctance to curb the news media, and the desire of the armed forces to inspire confidence and trust have combined to eliminate censorship

141

organization and procedures from U.S. military planning,
force structure, and capabilities.

Conclusions

Without a viable method to conduct censorship,
other measures must be used to permit media coverage of
combat operations by the U.S. armed forces. The following
discussion examines several wartime public affairs planning
issues and makes recommendations which would allow media
coverage of future operations:

The National Media Pool should be used for
contingency operations to areas of limited access to
western journalists. When a U.S. warfighting commander-
in-chief (CINC) recommends that sufficient journalists are
present in a theater of operations, and that the National
Media Pool should not deploy, this should mean that there
are correspondents present in the theater who have been
accredited to accompany U.S. forces into combat and who are
intended to accompany them. Therefore, each warfighting
CINC should develop a formal media pool of accredited
correspondents as a precursor to recommending that the
National Media Pool remain in Washington. Public Affairs
planning for contingency operations must be directed by the
Secretary of Defense with the understanding by all
warfighting CINCs that correspondents will accompany U.S.
forces into combat. The situation during the 1980s (in
Operations *Urgent Fury* and *Just Cause* for example) was that

the CINCs were told by the National Command Authorities not to let the media interfere with operations, only to almost invariably be directed to allow media participation hours before the operation began or even after the operation commenced. U.S. war planners spend years preparing contingency plans for any possible scenario but only have cursory plans for media access and support.

Ground rules should be formalized and published by the Department of Defense and supplemented by the warfighting CINC for specific operations. Accredited correspondents should be formally advised that ground rule violations will result in loss of accreditation and the accompanying loss of military access and support.

Accreditation systems should be formalized at the Department of Defense level and exercises should be conducted by the warfighting CINCs. Difficult policy decisions, i.e. should news media representatives be accredited regardless of nationality, must be formally addressed. As a condition of accreditation, correspondents should be asked to accompany U.S. forces during training or on exercise deployments to live in the field or on board surface combatants. Correspondents should learn first hand the requirements for anyone accompanying U.S. forces in combat. In return for this cooperation in issuing credentials, the warfighting CINCs should formalize planning which allows accredited correspondents to accompany U.S. forces on their operations immediately upon the outbreak of hostilities, and which allows them to transmit "pooled" news materials to media outlets.

Planning for military logistical support to correspondents should address access to military transport, communications, medical treatment, messing, billeting, equipment, work space, and graves registration. The experience of the U.S. armed forces in Vietnam is representative of future requirements for military logistical support to correspondents.

Military Assistance Command, Vietnam (MACV), accreditation offered correspondents covering that war a wealth of support. When away from Saigon hotels, for example, the armed forces arranged for correspondent billeting at little or no expense, whether the billet was a room in the visiting officer quarters in Da Nang or a cot in a tent in the field. In the field or in base camp messes, correspondents accompanying units usually ate "B" rations (hot meals) or "Meal-Combat-Individual" rations (C-rations) without charge.[20] Correspondents were authorized to purchase field equipment including uniform items, helmets, load-bearing equipment, and fragmentation vests at nominal cost or were issued the equipment without charge.[21]

Since no commercial communications services existed in country, correspondents were authorized military telephone service, including long-distance service, and teletype and courier services.[22] During the Vietnam conflict, precious rotary and fixed wing aircraft were dedicated exclusively to transport correspondents.[23] Even U.S. Army divisions typically dedicated helicopters for correspondents in the division area. Correspondents also routinely 'hitchhiked' on medevac and resupply helicopters and intratheater C-130 flights to cover stories in the field or to return to Saigon.[24]

MACV provided correspondents fully equipped press centers in each of the country's three regions. These centers provided lighted and air conditioned work rooms equipped with desks, military telephones, administrative supplies, typewriters and electrical outlets. The centers also contained briefing rooms. In the Saigon briefing room correspondents were briefed daily by MACV, in the 'Five O'Clock Follies,' on the progress of the war.[25]

Accredited correspondents were authorized 'emergency medical care not obtainable through local physicians' at military medical treatment facilities.[26] In addition, commanders of areas where correspondents became casualties were responsible for reporting the casualty and for 'disposing of the personal effects' of the dead.[27]

A significant burden to not only MACV but to corps and divisions in the field was a requirement to provide a military escort officer 'whenever reporters visited troops or covered operations.'[28] The U.S. provided escorts to an

145

average of about 40 U.S. correspondents and many other foreign journalists in the field at one time.[28]

Each logistical support issue must be addressed in future public affairs planning. The needed manpower, equipment and facilities will not materialize at the beginning of a conflict.

Access to logistical support through accreditation can be used to enforce ground rules. Accreditation can be revoked for violating ground rule or continued for obeying ground rules. In addition, accreditation can directly enforce ground rules by the security reviews of news material being sent over military communications or transportation or by a military escort officer restricting either a correspondent's access to sensitive operational information or the means of releasing that information.

The argument to restrict correspondents or control their reports from theaters of war is moot. News media coverage of combat operations by U.S. forces will occur. Planning and resources must be devoted to ensuring this coverage is adequate but does not endanger the mission of U.S. forces or cause unnecessary casualties. The effort should be guided by the sentiments of media planning during the latter stages of the Korean War: "We will proceed in the belief that the folks at home would rather get news a few hours late of a son who is living than news of a battle before it begins and then of a son who is dead."[30]

CHAPTER 7 ENDNOTES

1. U.S. Department of Defense, Defense Department Directives System Transmittal Cancellation Notice for Department of Defense Directive 5230.7, "Wartime Information Security Program (WISP)." Washington, D.C., 21 January 1987.

2. Peter Braestrop, *Battle Lines* (New York: Priority Press Publications, 1985), p. 95.

3. Mark Adkin, *Urgent Fury--The Battle for Grenada* (Lexington, Mass.: Lexington Books, 1989), pp. 258-59.

4. Joint Chiefs of Staff, *The Joint Operation Planning System-Volume I Deliberate Planning Procedures (SM209-83)*, Washington, D.C., 1983.

5. Maj. Barry E. Willey, U.S. Army, "Military Media Relations Come of Age," *Parameters* (19, No. 1, March 1989): 76-84.

6. Joint Chiefs of Staff, *The Joint Operation Planning System-Volume I Deliberate Planning Procedures (JCS Publication 5-02.1)*, Washington, D.C., 1988.

7. Col. Peter Alexandrakos, U.S. Air Force, Office of the Assistant Secretary of Defense (Public Affairs), Director for Plans, telephone interview, 21 March 1990.

8. Walter V. Robinson, "Journalists Constrained by Pentagon," *The Boston Globe*, 25 December 1989, p. 3; George Garneau, "Military Press Pool Misses Most of the Action," *Editor & Publisher*, 6 January 1990, pp. 4, 84; and Bruce van Voorst, "How Reporters Missed the War," *Time* (134, No. 2, 8 January 1990): 61.

9. Col. Peter Alexandrakos, U.S. Air Force, Office of the Assistant Secretary of Defense (Public Affairs), Director for Plans, telephone interview, 21 March 1990.

10. Ibid.

11. "VIASAT's Portable Satellite Terminal," *Telecommunications*, July 1989, pp. 68-69.

12. Ronald E. Rice, *The New Media: Communications, Research and Technology* (Beverly Hills: Sage, 1984), pp. 39-45; and U.S. Department of the Army, *Communications-*

*Electronics Fundamentals: Transmission Lines, Wave
Propagation, and Antennas (Field Manual 11-64)*, Washington,
D.C., 1985, pp. 3-1 to 3-4.

13. Ibid.

14. "Realtime Video Compression," *PC Week*, 6 March 1989, p.
69.

15. Rice, pp. 39-45.

16. Ibid.; and Tamara Bennett, "SATCOM Atop Everest."
reprint from *Satellite Communications Magazine*, May 1987.

17. Fred Hoffman, "Report on the Press Pool - Operation
Just Cause" (Unpublished report to the Assistant Secretary
of Defense (Public Affairs), Washington, D.C., March 1990.

18. "Armed Forces Communications and Electronics
Association Sustaining and Group Member Capabilities
Directory--Individual Company Listing 1989," *Signal* (43,
No. 6 February 1989): 177-358.

19. Hoffman.

20. Lieutenant General Joseph M. Heiser, Jr., U.S. Army,
Logistic Support, Vietnam Studies (Washington, D.C.: U.S.
Government Printing Office, 1974), p. 203.

21. U.S. Military Assistance Command, Vietnam, *Public
Information Policies and Procedures (Military Assistance
Command-Vietnam Directive 360-1)*, Saigon, 1967, pp. 13-14;
and U.S. Department of the Army, *Army Information Officers'
Guide (Department of the Army Pamphlet 360-5)*, Washington,
D.C., 1968, p. 8-3; and Phillip Knightley, *The First
Casualty* (New York: Harcourt, Brace, Jovanovich, 1976), p.
419; and Heiser, p. 208.

22. MACV Directive 360-1, p. 13; and Major General Thomas
M. Rienzi, U.S. Army, *Communications-Electronics 1962-1970*,
Vietnam Studies (Washington, D.C.: U.S. Government Printing
Office, 1972), pp. 42-43.

23. Hammond, p. 103.

24. Braestrup, *Battle Lines*, p. 64.

25. Hammond, p. 64.

26. MACV Directive 360-1, Annex F.

27. U.S. Department of the Army, *Army Information Officers' Guide (Department of the Army Pamphlet 360-5)*, p. 8-3.

28. Patricia A. Grossman, "The Future of Field Press Censorship: Is There One?" Unpublished student paper, U.S. Army War College, Carlisle Barracks, Pa., 1989, p. 14.

29. Braestrup, *Battle Lines*, pp. 64-65.

30. Lieutenant Colonel Melvin B. Voorhees, U.S. Army, *Korean Tales* (New York: Simon and Schuster, 1952), p. 102.

APPENDIX 1

APPENDIX 1

U.S. WARTIME PRESS CENSORSHIP DOCUMENTS FROM WORLD WAR I

Committee on Public Information's
December 1917 Voluntary Censorship Restrictions

The following is the text of the Committee on Public Information's voluntary censorship restrictions issued in December 1917:*

THE NEW REQUESTS IN FULL

Following are the new requests in full:

The desires of the Government with respect to the concealment from the enemy of military policies, plans and movements are set forth in the following specific requests. They go to the press of the United States directly from the Secretaries of War and the Navy, and represent the thought and advice of their technical advisers. They do not apply to news dispatches censored by military authority with the Expeditionary Forces or in those cases where the Government itself, in the form of official statements, may find it necessary or expedient to make public information covered by these requests.

For the protection of our military and naval forces and of merchant shipping it is requested that secrecy be observed in all matters of:

1. Advance information of the routes and schedules of troop movements. (See paragraph 5.)

---

*Harold L. Nelson, ed., *Freedom of the Press from Hamilton to the Warren Court* (Indianapolis: Bobbs-Merrill, 1967), p. 253.

2. Information tending to disclose the number of troops in the Expeditionary Forces abroad.

3. Information calculated to disclose location of the permanent base or bases abroad.

4. Information that would disclose the location of American units or the eventual position of the American forces at the front.

PORTS OF EMBARKATION

5. Information tending to disclose an eventual or actual port of embarkation; or information of the movement of military forces toward seaports or of the assembling of military forces at seaports form which inference might be drawn of any intention to embark them for service abroad; and information of the assembling of transports or convoys; and information of the embarkation itself.

6. Information of the arrival at any European port of American war vessels, transports, or any portion of any expeditionary force, combatant or noncombatant.

7. Information of the time of departure of merchant ships from American or European ports, or information of the ports from which they sailed, or information of their cargoes.

8. Information indicating the port of arrival of incoming ships from European ports or after their arrival indicating, or hinting at, the port at which the ship arrived.

9. Information as to convoys and as to the sighting of friendly or enemy ships, whether naval or merchant.

10. Information of the locality, number, or identity of vessels belonging to our Navy or to the navies of any country at war with Germany.

11. Information of the coast or anti-aircraft defenses of the United States. Any information of their very existence, as well as the number, nature, or position of their guns, is dangerous.

MINES AND HARBOR DEFENSES

12. Information on the laying of mines or mine fields or of any harbor defenses.

13. Information of the aircraft and appurtenances used at Government aviation schools for experimental tests under military authority, and information of contracts and production of air material, and information tending to disclose the numbers and organization of the air division, excepting when authorized by the Committee on Public Information.

14. Information of all Government devices and experiments in war material, excepting when authorized by the Committee on Public Information.

15. Information of secret notices issued to mariners or other confidential instructions issued by the Navy or Department of Commerce relating to lights, lightships, buoys, or other guides to navigation.

16. Information as to the number, size, character, or location of ships of the Navy ordered laid down at any port or shipyard, or in actual process of construction; or information that they are launched or in commission.

17. Information of the train or boat schedules of traveling official missions in transit through the United States.

18. Information of the transportation of munitions, or of war material.

PHOTOGRAPHS

Photographs conveying the information specified above should not be published.

These requests go to the press without larger authority than the necessities of the war-making branches. Their enforcement is a matter of the press itself. To the overwhelming proportion of newspapers, who have given unselfish, patriotic adherence to the voluntary agreement, the Government extends its gratitude and high appreciation.

APPENDIX 2

APPENDIX 2

U.S. WARTIME PRESS CENSORSHIP DOCUMENTS FROM WORLD WAR II

OFFICE OF CENSORSHIP PRESS CODE

The following is the text of the U.S. Office of Censorship Press Code issued on 15 January 1942, with revisions issued 25 June 1942 enclosed in parentheses:*

It is essential that certain basic facts be understood. The first of these facts is that the outcome of the war is a matter of vital personal concern to the future of every American citizen. The second is that the security of our armed forces and even of our homes and our liberties will be weakened in greater or less degree by every disclosure of information which will help the enemy.

If every member of every news staff and contributing writer will keep these two facts constantly in mind, and then will follow the dictates of common sense. he will be able to answer for himself many of the questions which might otherwise trouble him. In other words a maximum of accomplishment will be attained if editors will ask themselves with respect to any given detail: 'Is this information I would like to have if I were the enemy?' and then act accordingly.

The result of such a process will hardly represent 'business as usual' on the news desks of the country. On the contrary, it will mean some sacrifice of the journalistic enterprise of ordinary times. But it will not mean a news or editorial blackout. It is the hope and expectation of the Office of Censorship that the columns of American publications will remain the freest in the world and will tell the story of our national successes and shortcomings accurately and in much detail.

The highly gratifying response of the press so far proves that it understands the need for temporary sacrifice and is prepared to make that sacrifice in the spirit of the President's assurance that such curtailment as may be necessary will be administered 'in harmony with the best

---

*Quoted in Robert E. Summers, ed., *Wartime Censorship of Press and Radio* (New York: H. W. Wilson, 1942), pp. 259-66.

interests of our free institutions.'

Below is a summary covering specific problems.
This summary repeats, with some modifications, requests
previously made by various agencies of the Federal
Government, and it may be regarded as superseding and
consolidating all of these requests.

(Obviously it is impossible to anticipate every
conceivable contingency. The Office of Censorship will
make special requests from time to time covering individual
situations in order to round out this outline of newspaper
and magazine practices which the government feels are
desirable for the effective prosecution of the war and the
security of American citizens.)

Special attention is directed to the fact that all
of the requests in the summary are modified by a proviso
that the information listed may properly be published when
authorized by appropriate authority. News on all of these
subjects will become available from government sources; but
in war, timeliness is an important factor, and the
government unquestionably is in the best position to decide
when disclosure is timely.

The specific information which newspapers,
magazines and all other media of publication are asked not
to publish except when such information is made available
officially by appropriate authority falls into the
following classes:

TROOPS

The general character and movements of United
States Army, Navy, and Marine Corps units, within or
without the continental limits of the United States--their
location, identity, or exact composition, equipment, or
strength; destination, routes, and schedules; assembly for
embarkation, prospective embarkation, or actual
embarkation. Any such information regarding the troops of
friendly nations on American soil.

Note--The request as regards 'location' and
'general character' does not apply to troops in training
camps in continental United States nor to units assigned to
domestic police duty. (Names and addresses of troops in
domestic camps may be published, if they do not give the
location of units disposed for tactical purposes or predict
troop movements or embarkations. Names of naval personnel
should not be linked with their ships or bases. Names of
individuals stationed in combat areas outside the United
States may be published after there has been official
announcement of the presence of American troops in such
areas. No mention should be made of their military units.
Possible future military operations should not be revealed
by identifying an individual known for a specialized

activity.)

SHIP MOVEMENTS, CARGOES, ETC.

(The identity, location and movements of United
States naval or merchant vessels, of neutral vessels, or
vessels of nations opposing the Axis powers in any waters,
unless such information is made public outside continental
United States; the port and time of arrival or prospective
cargoes of such vessels; the identity or location of enemy
naval or merchant vessels in any waters, unless such
information is made public outside continental United
States; the identity, assembly, or movements of transports
or convoys; the existence of mine fields or other harbor
defenses; secret orders or other secret instructions
regarding lights, buoys and other guides to navigators; the
number, size, character and location of ships in
construction, or advance information as to the date of
launchings or commissionings; the physical set-up or
technical details of shipyards.)

(Note--This has no reference to the movement of
merchant vessels on the Great Lakes or other sheltered
inland waterways, unless specific instances require special
rulings.)

SHIP SINKINGS, DAMAGE BY ENEMY ATTACKS, ETC.

(Information about the sinking or damaging from war
causes of war or merchant vessels in any waters, unless
such information is made public outside the United States,
and its origin stated.)

(Note--The appropriate authority for the release of
news about the sinking or damaging of American naval or
merchant vessels in or near American waters is the Naval
Office of Public Relations, Washington; for results of
United States naval action against enemy vessels in or near
American waters, the commanding officer of the district in
which the action occurs, or the Naval Office of Public
Relations, Washington.)

(Information about damage to military objectives,
including docks, railroads, airfields, or public utilities
or industrial plants engaged in war work, through enemy
land or sea attacks on continental United States or
possessions.)

(Note--In reporting such attacks, counter-measures
or plans of defense should not be disclosed, except through
appropriate military authorities.)

(The appropriate authority for information about
damage from enemy attacks to military objectives on land
within continental United States or possessions is the
commanding officer in the zone of combat or the Army Bureau

157

of Public Relations, Washington. For the Hawaiian Islands,
the Navy.)

ATTACKS BY AIR

(To the end that any air attack on continental
United States may be reported in an orderly fashion,
consistent with the highest requirements of national
security, the following course of action before, during and
after an air raid is suggested;)

(Before a raid--It is desirable that no warning or
report of an impending raid be published except as given
out by designated representatives of the Army Defense
Command.)

(Note--It is suggested that newspapers write in
advance to the appropriate defense commander to ascertain
the location of the designated representatives of the
defense command in their area.)

(During a raid--It is requested that news
dispatches transmitted or published at the beginning of a
raid, prior to official announcement, be confined to the
following: (1) the fact that a raid has begun, without
estimating the number of planes; (2) the fact that some
bombs have been dropped, if fully established, but without
effort to estimate the number; (3) the bare fact that anti-
aircraft guns have gone into action.)

(Thereafter, until the raid is ended and the all-
clear sounded, it is requested that nothing be transmitted
or published except communiques, which will become
available promptly and periodically from the designated
representatives of the Army Defense Command.)

(After a raid--There is no objection to publication
of general descriptions of the action after the all-clear
is given, provided such accounts do not (1) play up horror
or sensationalism; (2) deal with or refer to unconfirmed
versions or reports; (3) contain any estimate of the number
of planes involved or the number of bombs dropped except as
given in communiques; (4) make any reference to damage to
military objectives such as fortifications, docks,
railroads, ships, airfields, public utilities, or
industrial plants engaged in war work; (5) make any mention
of the exact routes taken by enemy planes; (6) describe
counter-measures of defense, such as troop mobilizations or
movements, or the number or location of anti-aircraft guns
or searchlights 'n action, except as officially announced.)

(It is requested that no photographs showing damage
or combat action be published or transmitted except upon
clearance by military authorities.)

(Nothing in this request is intended to prevent or
curtail constructive reporting of such matters as feats of
heroism, incidents of personal courage, or response to duty

by the military or by civilian defense workers.)

PLANES

(Disposition, movements, missions, new characteristics, or strength of military air units of the United States or the United Nations unless such information is made public outside the continental United States and its origin stated; scope and extent of military activities and missions of the Civil Air Patrol; movements of personnel, material, or other activities by commercial air lines for the military services, including changes of schedules occasioned thereby.)

(Activities, operations and installations of the air forces Ferrying Command, the R.A.F Ferrying Command, or commercial companies operating services for or in cooperation with the Ferrying Command.)

(Information concerning new military aircraft and related items of equipment or detailed information on performance, construction and armament of current military aircraft or related items now in service or commercial airline planes in international traffic.)

FORTIFICATIONS

(The location of forts, and other fortifications; the location of coast-defense emplacements, anti-aircraft guns, and other defense installations; their nature and number; location of bomb shelters; location of camouflaged objects; information concerning installations by American military units outside the continental United States.)

PRODUCTION

(Specifications which saboteurs could use to gain access to or damage war-production plants.)

(Exact estimates of the amount, schedules or delivery date of future production, or exact reports of current production.)

(Exact amounts involved in new contracts for war production, and the specific nature or specifications of such production.)

(Note--Information about the award of contracts is proper for publication when officially announced by the War Production Board, or by the government agency responsible for executing the contract, or when disclosed in public records.)

(Nature of production should be generalized as follows: tanks, planes, plane parts, motorized vehicles, uniform equipment, ordnance, munitions, vessels. Generalize all types of camps to `camps` or `cantonments.`)

159

(Any statistical information other than officially
issued by a proper government department which would
disclose the amounts of strategic of critical materials
produced, imported, or in reserve--such as tin, rubber,
aluminum, uranium, zinc, chromium, manganese, tungsten,
silk, platinum, cork, quinine, copper, optical glass,
mercury, high-octane gasoline.)

(Any information indicating industrial sabotage.
In reporting industrial accidents, no mention of sabotage
should be made unless cleared with the appropriate military
authority.)

(Any information about new or secret military
designs, formulas, or experiments; secret manufacturing
processes or secret factory designs, either for war
production or capable of adaptation for war production.)

(Nationwide or regional round-ups of current war
production or war contract procurement data; local round-
ups disclosing total numbers of war production plants and
the nature of their production.)

WEATHER

Weather forecasts, other than officially issued by
the Weather Bureau; the routine forecasts printed by any
single newspaper to cover only the State in which it is
published and not more than four adjoining States, portions
of which lie within a radius of 150 miles from the point of
publication.

Consolidated temperature tables covering more than
twenty stations in any one newspaper.

(Note--Any news stories about weather occurrences
within the State of publication, and outside the State for
an area not to exceed 150 miles from the point of the news
stories about weather occurrences, especially extremes such
as blizzards, snowstorms, hurricanes, tornadoes and floods
for areas other than the foregoing will be appropriate for
publication only when specifically cleared through the
Office of Censorship. Effects of weather conditions on
sports events are appropriate for publication when used
briefly to describe the condition of the grounds, or as
reasons for postponing matches, such as "Muddy Field," "Wet
Grounds" or "Game Called Because of Weather." Specific
mention of such conditions as "rain," "overcast," "windy,"
"clear," or "sudden temperature drop" should be avoided.)

NOTES ON RUMORS

The spread of rumors in such a way that they will
be accepted as facts will render aid and comfort to the
enemy. (The same is true of enemy propaganda or material
calculated by the enemy to bring about division among the

United Nations. Enemy claims of ship sinkings, or of other
damage to our forces should be weighed carefully and the
sources clearly identified, if published. Equal caution
should be used in handling so-called 'atrocity' stories.)
(Interviews with service men or civilians from
combat zones should be submitted for authority to the
Office of Censorship or to the appropriate Army or Navy
Public Relations officer.)

PHOTOGRAPHS AND MAPS

(Photographs conveying the information specified in
this summary including ports of embarkation, embarking
troops, harbor views of convoys, military air fields in
continental United States completed after Dec. 7, 1941, or
emergency airfields no matter when completed; harbor
defenses; inland waterway locks.)
(Special care should be exercised in the
publication of aerial photos presumably of non-military
significance, which might reveal military or other
information helpful to the enemy; also care should be
exercised in publishing casualty photos so as not to reveal
unit identifications through collar ornaments, etc.
Special attention is directed to the section of this
summary covering information about damage to military
objectives.)
(Maps disclosing the location of military depots of
any kind, such as air, quartermaster or ordnance depots;
key war production plants; arsenals; ammunition or
explosive plants of any kind.)
(Note--This has no reference to maps showing the
general theater of war or large-scale zones of action,
movements of contending forces on a large scale, or maps
showing the general ebb and flow of battle lines; or maps
showing locations of military camps, provided no indication
is given of size or strength, or maps showing airfields,
except those constructed after Dec. 7, 1941.)

GENERAL CASUALTY LISTS

(Note--There is no objection to publication of
information about casualties from a newspaper's local
field, obtained from nearest of kin, but it is requested
that in such cases, specific military units and exact
locations be not mentioned.)
(There is no objection to identifying naval
casualties with their ships, after such ships have been
officially reported damaged or lost.)
Information disclosing the new location of national
archives, or of public (or private) art treasures.
(Names of persons arrested, questioned, or interned

as enemy aliens; names of persons moved to resettlement centers; location and description of places of internment and resettlement.

(Note--The Department of Justice or the Provost Marshal General is the appropriate authority for disclosing names of persons arrested, questioned, or interned as enemy aliens; the official in charge, for names of persons moved to resettlement centers; the Office of Censorship, for location and description of internment camps; the official in charge, for location and description of resettlement centers.)

(Information about production, amounts, dates and method of delivery, destination or routes, of lend-lease war material.)

(Premature disclosure of diplomatic negotiations or conversations.)

Information about the movement of munitions or other war materials.

Information about the movement of the President of the United States or official military or diplomatic missions of the United States or of any other nation opposing the Axis powers--routes, schedules, destination, within or without continental United States; movements of ranking Army or Navy officers and staffs on official missions; movements of other individuals or units (on military or diplomatic missions.)

(Note--All requests in the code apply to advertising matter, news letters, corporation reports, letters to the editor, personal and society news [which often discloses identity or movement of activity] columns, etc.)

If information concerning any phase of the war effort should be made available anywhere which seems to come from doubtful authority, or to be in conflict with the general aims of these requests; or if special restrictions requested locally or otherwise by various authorities seem unreasonable or out of harmony with this summary, it is recommended that the question be submitted at once to the Office of Censorship.

In addition, if any newspaper, magazine, or other agency or individual handling news or special articles desires clarification or advice as to what disclosures might or might not aid the enemy, the Office of Censorship will cooperate gladly. Such inquiries should be addressed to the Office of Censorship, Washington. Telephone Executive 3800.

Should further additions or modifications of this summary seem feasible and desirable from time to time, the industry will be advised.

The Office of Censorship,
Byron Price, Director.

CONFIDENTIAL PRESS AND RADIO CODE SUPPLEMENT

The following is the text of a confidential message sent to 25,000 U.S. editors and broadcasters by Byron Price on 28 June 1943:*

      The Code of Wartime Practices for the American Press and American Broadcasters request that nothing be published or broadcast about 'new or secret military weapons . . . experiments.' In extension of this highly vital precaution, you are asked not to publish or broadcast any information whatever regarding war experiments involving:
      Production or utilization of atom smashing, atomic energy, atomic fission, atomic splitting, or any of their equivalents.
      The use for military purposes of radium or radioactive materials, heavy water, high voltage discharge equipment, cyclotrons.
      The following elements or any of their compounds: polonium, uranium, ytterbium, hafnium, protactinium, radium, rhenium, thorium, deuterium.

---

    *As quoted in Theodore F. Koop, *Weapon of Silence* (Chicago: University of Chicago Press, 1946), pp. 274-75.

OFFICE OF CENSORSHIP REVISED RADIO CODE

The following is the text of the U.S. Office of Censorship Revised Radio Code issued on 24 June 1942:*

Five months have passed since the Office of Censorship issued the Code of Wartime Practices for American Broadcasters. This is a revision of that Code, combining original provisions with supplemental suggestions and interpretations which have developed out of our experience in working with the broadcast industry.

The broad approach to the problem of voluntary censorship remains unchanged. In sum, this approach is that it is the responsibility of every American to help prevent the dissemination of information which will be of value to the enemy and inimical to the war effort. It is true now, as it was five months ago, that the broadcasting industry must be awake to the dangers inherent in (1) news broadcasts and (2) routine programming.

To combat these dangers effectively, broadcast management must be in complete control of all programming every minute of every day of operation. That accomplished--the broadcasting industry will have fulfilled an important wartime obligation.

Radio station managements will continue to function as their own censors. The facilities of the Office of Censorship are at their disposal 24 hours a day to assist them with consultation and advice when any doubt arises as to the application of this Code. The following are the principal advisory guideposts which are intended to aid them in discharging their censorship responsibilities.

I. NEWS BROADCASTS

Radio, because of the international character of its transmissions, should edit all news broadcasts in the light of this Code's suggestions, and of its own specialized knowledge, regardless of the medium or means through which such news is obtained.

---

*Quoted in Robert E. Summers, ed., *Wartime Censorship of Press and Radio* (New York: H. W. Wilson, 1942), pp. 266-79.

It is requested that news of any of the following classifications be kept off the air, unless released or authorized for release by appropriate authority.

(a) Weather

All weather data, either forecasts, summaries, recapitulations, or details of weather conditions.

Stations should refrain from broadcasting any news relating to the results of weather phenomena such as tornadoes, hurricanes, storms, etc., unless it is specifically authorized for broadcast by the Office of Censorship. Occasionally, it is possible to clear such news, but for security reasons this office cannot authorize blanket clearance in advance.

Each case must be considered individually in the light of the extent to which the enemy will be benefitted if such information is broadcast. Confusion and inequalities of competition can be avoided if stations will consult the Office of Censorship promptly in all such cases, either directly or through their news service.

Exceptions: Emergency warnings when specifically released for broadcast by Weather Bureau authorities.

Announcements regarding flood conditions may be broadcast provided they contain no reference to weather conditions.

Information concerning hazardous road conditions may be broadcast when requested by a Federal, State or Municipal source, if it avoids reference to the weather.

(Note: Special events reporters covering sports events are cautioned against the mention of weather conditions in describing contests, announcing their schedules, suspensions, or cancellations.)

(b) Troops

Type and movements of United States Army, Navy and Marine Corps Units, within or without continental United States, including information concerning

> Location
> Identity
> Composition
> Equipment
> Strength
> Routes
> Schedules
> Assembly for Embarkation
> Prospective Embarkation
> Actual Embarkation
> Destination

Such information regarding troops of friendly nations on American soil.

Revelation of possible future military operations by identifying an individual known for a specialized activity.

Exceptions: Troops in training camps in United States and units assigned to domestic police duty, as regards location and general character. Names, addresses of troops in domestic camps (if they do not give location of units disposed for tactical purposes or predict troop movements or embarkations). Names of individuals stationed in combat areas outside the United States (after presence of American troops in area has been announced and if their military units are not identified). Names of naval personnel should not be linked with their ships or bases.
(c) Ships (Convoys, etc.)

Type and movements of United States Navy, or merchant vessels, or transports, or convoys, of neutral vessels of nations opposing the Axis powers in any waters, including information concerning

        Identity
        Location
        Port of Arrival
        Time of Arrival
        Prospect of Arrival
        Port of Departure
        Ports of Call
        Nature of Cargoes
        Assembly
        Personnel

Enemy naval or merchant vessels in any waters, their

        Type
        Identity
        Location
        Movements

Secret information or instructions about set defenses, such as

        Buoys, lights and other guides to navigators
        Mine fields and other harbor defenses

Ship construction

        Type
        Number
        Size
        Advance information on dates of launchings, commissionings
        Physical description, technical details of shipyards

Exceptions: Information made public outside the United States and origin stated. Movements of merchant vessels on Great Lakes or other sheltered inland waterways unless specific instances require special ruling.
(d) Damage by Enemy Land or Sea Attacks

Information on damage to military objectives in continental United States or possessions, including

        Docks
        Railroads

                    Airfields
                    Public Utilities
                    Industrial plants engages in war work
          Counter-measures or plans of defense
(e) Action at Sea
          Information about the sinking or damaging of navy,
or merchant vessels or transports in any waters.
          Exceptions: Information made public outside United
States and origin stated.
          Appropriate authority: For news about naval action
against United States vessels in or near American waters:
Naval Office of Public Relations; by United States vessels
or aircraft against the enemy in or near American waters:
Naval commander in district where action occurs or Naval
Office of Public Relations, Washington.
(f) Enemy Air Attacks
          Estimates of number of planes involved; number of
bombs dropped; damage to
                    Fortifications
                    Docks
                    Railroads
                    Ships
                    Airfields
                    Public Utilities
                    Industrial Plants engaged in war work
                    All other military objectives
          Warnings or reports of impending air raid; remote
ad lib broadcasts dealing with raids, during or after the
action.
          Mention of raid in the continental United States
during its course by stations outside the zone of action,
unless expressly announced for broadcast by the War
Department in Washington.
          News which plays up horror or sensationalism; deals
with or refers to unconfirmed reports or versions; refers
to exact routes taken by enemy planes, or describes
counter-measures of defense such as troop mobilization or
movements, or the number and location of anti-aircraft guns
or searchlights in action.
          Exceptions: After an air raid, general
descriptions of action after all-clear has been given.
Nothing in this request is intended to prevent or curtail
constructive reporting or programming of such matters as
feats of heroism, incidents of personal courage, or
response to duty by the military or by civilian defense
workers.
(g) Planes
          Air Units--Military air units of the United States
and the United Nations as to
                    Disposition
                    Missions

                         167

Movements
New Characteristics
Strength

Aircraft--New or current military aircraft or
information concerning their
Armament
Construction
Performance
Equipment
Cargo

Civil Air Patrol--Nature and extent of military
activities and missions.

Miscellaneous--Movements of personnel or material
or other activities by commercial airlines for military
purposes, including changes of schedules occasioned
thereby.

Activities, operations and installations of United
States and United Nations Air Forces Ferrying Commands, or
commercial companies operating services for, or in
cooperation with such Ferrying Commands.

Commercial airline planes in international traffic.

Exceptions: When made public outside continental
United States and origin stated.

(h) Fortifications and Bases

The location of forts, other fortifications, their
nature and number, including
Anti-aircraft guns
Barrage balloons and all other air defense
installations
Bomb shelters
Camouflaged objects
Coast-defense emplacements

Information concerning installations by American
military units outside the continental United States.

Exceptions: None.

(i) Production

Plants--Specifications which saboteur could use to
gain access to or damage war production plants.

Exact estimates of the amount, schedules, or
delivery date of future production or exact reports of
current production

Contracts--Exact amounts involved in new contracts
for war production and the specific nature of the
specifications of such production.

Statistics--Any statistical information which would
disclose the amounts of strategic or critical materials
produced, imported or in reserve, such as tin, rubber,
aluminum, uranium, zinc, chromium, manganese, tungsten,
silk, platinum, cork, quinine, copper, optical glasses,
mercury, high octane gasoline. Disclosure of movements of
such materials and of munitions.

168

Sabotage--Information indicating sabotage in reporting industrial accidents.

Secret Designs--Any information about new or secret military designs, formulas, or experiments, secret manufacturing, either for war production or capable of adaptation for war production.

Roundups--Nation-wide or regional roundups of current war production or war contract procurement data; local round-ups disclosing total numbers of war production plants and the nature of their production.

Type of Production--Nature of production should be generalized as follows: tanks, planes, parts, motorized vehicles, uniform equipment, ordnance, munitions, vessels.

Exceptions: Information about the award of contracts when officially announced by the War Production Board, the government agency executing the contract, a member of Congress, or when disclosed in public records.

(j) Unconfirmed Reports, Rumors

The spread of rumors in such way that they will be accepted as facts will render aid and comfort to the enemy. The same is true of enemy propaganda or material calculated by the enemy to bring about division among the United Nations. Enemy claims of ship sinkings, or of other damage to our forces should be weighed carefully and the sources clearly identified, if broadcast. Equal caution should be used in handling so-called 'atrocity' stories. Interviews with Service men or civilians from combat zones should be submitted for authority either to the Office of Censorship or to the appropriate Army or Navy public relations officer.

(k) Communications

Information concerning the establishment of new international points of communication.

(l) General

Aliens--Names of persons arrested, questioned or interned as enemy aliens; names of persons moved to resettlement centers; location and description of internment camps; location and description of resettlement centers.

Art Objects, Historical Data--Information disclosing the new location of national archives, or of public or private art treasures.

Casualties--Mention of specific military units and exact locations in broadcasting information about casualties from a station's primary area, as obtained from nearest of kin. Identification of naval casualties with their ships, unless such ships have been officially reported damaged or lost.

Diplomatic Information--Information about the movement of the President of the United States or of official, military or diplomatic missions or agents of the

United States or of any nation opposing the Axis powers--
routes, schedules, destinations within or without
continental United States. Premature disclosure of
diplomatic negotiations or conversations.

        Lend-Lease War Material--Information about
production, amounts, dates and method of delivery,
destination or routes, of Lend-Lease war material.

        Exceptions--None.

II. PROGRAMS

        The following suggestions are made in order that
broadcasters will have a pattern to follow in accomplishing
the most important censorship function of program
operation: keeping the microphone under the complete
control of the station management, or its authorized
representative.

(a) Request Programs

        Music--No telephoned or telegraphed requests for
musical selections should be accepted.

        No requests for musical selections made by word-of-
mouth at the origin of broadcast, whether studio or remote,
should be honored.

        Talk--No telephoned or telegraphed requests for
service announcements should be honored, except as
hereinafter qualified. Such service announcements would
include information relating to:

                Lost pets
                'Swap' ads
                Mass meetings
                Club meetings
                Club programs, etc.

        No telephoned, telegraphed or word-of-mouth
dedications of program features or segments thereof should
be broadcast.

        Exceptions--Emergency announcements (such as those
seeking blood donors, doctors, lost persons, lost property,
etc.) may be handled in conventional manner if the
broadcaster confirms their origin. They should emanate
from the police, the Red Cross, or similar recognized
governmental or civilian agencies.

        Service announcements may be honored when source is
checked and material is submitted in writing, subject to
rewriting by station and continuity staff. Requests for
the broadcast of greetings or other programs to commemorate
personal anniversaries may be honored on the anniversary
date or at the time or on the date designated in the
requests. These and all requests may be honored when
submitted via mail, or otherwise in writing if they are
held for an unspecified length of time and if the

broadcaster staggers the order in which such requests are honored, rewriting any text which may be broadcast.

(b) Quiz Programs

It is requested that all audience-participation type quiz programs originating from remote points, either by wire, transcription or short wave be discontinued, except as qualified hereinafter. Any program which permits the public accessibility to an open microphone is dangerous and should be carefully supervised.

Because of the nature of quiz programs, in which the public is not only permitted access to the microphone but encouraged to speak into it, the danger of usurpation by the enemy is enhanced. The greater danger here lies in the informal interview conducted in a small group--10 to 25 people. In larger groups, where participants are selected from a theater audience, for example, the danger is not so great.

Generally speaking, any quiz program originating remotely, wherein the group is small, wherein no arrangement exists for investigating the background of participants, and wherein extraneous background noises cannot be eliminated at the discretion of the broadcaster, should be discontinued. Included in this classification are all such productions as man-in-the-street interviews, airport interviews, train terminal interviews, and so forth.

In all studio-audience type quiz shows, where the audience from which interviewees are to be selected numbers less than 50 people, program conductors are asked to exercise special care. They should devise a method whereby no individual seeking participation can be guaranteed participation.

(c) Forums and Interviews.

During forums in which the general public is permitted extemporaneous comment, panel discussions in which more than two persons participate, and interviews conducted by authorized employees of the broadcasting company, broadcasters should devise method guaranteeing against the release of any information which might aid the enemy as described in Section I of the Code. If there is doubt concerning the acceptability of material to be used in interviews, complete scripts should be submitted to the Office of Censorship for reviews.

(d) Commentaries (ad lib)

Special events reporters should study carefully the restrictions suggested in Section I of the Code, especially those referring to interviews and descriptions following enemy action. Reporters and commentators should guard against use of descriptive material which might be employed by the enemy in plotting an area for attack.

If special programs which might be considered doubtful enterprises in view of our effort to keep information of value from the enemy are planned, outlines should be submitted to the Office of Censorship for review.

Caution is advised against reporting, under the guise of opinion, speculation or prediction, any fact which has not been released by an appropriate authority.

(e) Dramatic Programs

Radio is requested to avoid dramatic programs which attempt to portray the horrors of war, and sound effects which might be mistaken for air raid alarms, or for any other defense alarm.

(f) Commercial Continuity

Broadcasters should be alert to prevent the transmission of subversive information through the use of commercial continuity in program or announcement broadcasts.

In this connection, the continuity editor should regard his responsibility as equal to that of the news editor.

(g) Foreign Language Programs

Broadcasters have recognized that the loyalty of their personnel is of supreme importance in voluntary censorship; they recognize the dangers inherent in those foreign language broadcasts which are not under the control of all times of responsible station executives. Station managements, therefore, are requested to require all persons who broadcast in a foreign language to submit to the management in advance of broadcast complete scripts or transcripts of such material, with an English translation. It is further requested that such material be checked `on the air` against the approved script, and that no deviation therefrom be permitted. These scripts or transcriptions with their translations should be kept on file at the station.

Broadcasters should ask themselves, `Is this information of value to the enemy?` If the answer is `yes,` they should not use it. If doubtful, they should measure the material against the Code.

If information concerning any phase of the war effort should be made available anywhere, which seems to come from doubtful authority, or to be in conflict with the general aims of these requests; or if special restrictions requested locally or otherwise by various authorities seem unreasonable or out of harmony with this summary, it is recommended that the question be submitted at once to the Office of Censorship.

<u>THE FIRST NATIONAL ASSOCIATION OF BROADCASTERS</u>
<u>WAR SERVICE BULLETIN</u>

The following is the text of the first National Association
of Broadcasters War Service Bulletin, issued on behalf of
the Federal Communications Commission to all broadcasters
on 9 December 1941:*

STATION SILENCES

The Federal Communications Commission announces
that at the request of the army, it has assigned field
inspectors to perform liaison duties between the
Interceptor Command and the commercial radio stations in
each area where radio silence may be required. When the
inspector directs a station to maintain radio silence, it
should be understood that the order originated with the
Interceptor Command of the Army and carries with it the
authority of the Federal Communications Commission.
Radio stations will be advised as promptly as
possible, when radio silence is no longer required so that
they may resume normal operations. In this connection,
plans are being made to effect a more rapid system of
communication between the Commission's inspectors and the
radio stations which may be required to go off the air.

WAIT FOR FACTS

Don't broadcast 'unconfirmed reports.'
Don't broadcast rumors.
This should apply whether your own news staff has
gathered these 'unconfirmed reports' or whether they come
from the news services.
Wait for the facts. This is part of your
responsibility for civilian morale.

PROGRAM CAUTIONS

---

*Quoted in Robert E. Summers, ed., *Wartime Censorship
of Press and Radio* (New York: H. W. Wilson, 1942), *pp.* 279-
82.

The War Department has pointed out the need for the exercise of extreme care in the handling of all news and the opportunities for facts to reach the air, and this involves even the innocent looking quiz type show or man in the street broadcast. For example, in a seaport city a man on the street announcer on the air noticed a little girl in the crowd. He asked her name and she told him. He asked where she was going and this is what she said. 'I am going to the Navy Yard. My Mummy just got a call from my brother,' and the announcer said, 'What is that package under your arm?' She replied, 'Mummy is sending some cakes and cookies to my brother before he leaves.' The announcer then asked, 'Where is he going?' and she said immediately to be heard by the entire radio audience, 'He is going to Iceland and I'd better hurry because he told Mummy the boat was leaving in an hour.'

The War Department points out that this information could have led to the loss of American lives on a transport for it would be relayed by any enemy agents who were monitoring the station.

This is what we mean when we say that caution should be exercised not only in what we ourselves do but in permitting an opportunity, however inadvertent, for such information to reach the air.

The War Department points out that with the establishment of a system of daily communiques stations will no doubt find it possible and desirable to bring about a more orderly handling of the war news at definite periods of time rather than the constant interruption of program service which has the effect of keeping people (who should be working) listening to the radio all day long. If these people knew that at stated intervals of time they could hear the latest war news it would materially assist the establishment of a stable and orderly civilian morale.

The N.A.B. is in hearty agreement with this.

WAR DEPARTMENT POINTERS

The following memorandum went out December 8 from the War Department to all broadcasters. On December 9, Point 1, regarding casualty lists, and Point 3, regarding station protection, were modified. Be sure to read the modifications, following this memorandum.

In line with the cooperation of Radio News Wire Services with the Radio Branch of the War Department, the following is for your information and we request immediate transmissions to your radio clients:

1. Broadcast of casualty lists.

No casualty lists will be released until the nearest of kin have been notified; they will be available

for immediate broadcast, upon release, from this wire. To
eliminate undue anxiety, however, it is suggested that only
names of persons in your immediate listening area be
broadcast. No network will broadcast complete lists,
although newspapers will publish them. Names of
casualties, when released, should be broadcast in regular
newscast periods or in groups in time set aside for that
purpose and not as flashes, interrupting regular program
service. Rumors of casualties should not be broadcast. No
surmises of persons believed to be on casualty lists should
be broadcast until officially confirmed in official
releases from the War Department.

2.   Broadcasting secret information.
        Reemphasizing the statement of Secretary Stimson
made Sunday concerning restriction on the broadcast or
publication of information regarding the strength,
positions, or movements of United States troops, outside
the continental limits of the United States. This
statement also covers all troop movements in the United
States or to outlying posts unless same is officially
announced.

3.   Transmitter protection.
        Station managers desiring military protection of
transmitters should immediately contact the Commanding
Officer of the Corps Area in which transmitter is located.
(Consult map in relation map in relation to Radio Station
and Corps Areas, distributed by N.A.B.)

4.   State news editor's groups.
        District N.A.B. directors are requested to send to
E. M. Kirby, Chief, Radio Branch, War Department,
immediately names of state chairmen of news editors and
program directors groups as set up at recent district
N.A.B. meetings.

5.   News releases.
        The War and Navy Departments soon will establish a
regular schedule of official communiques, possibly for
release twice daily so that broadcasters may present war
news in a more orderly scheduled manner.

                    AS TO CASUALTIES

        We are requested to transmit the following
statement signed by Ed Kirby, Radio Branch, War Department,
and addressed to all radio stations:

        "We have just been informed by the National
Association of Broadcasters that it is advising

radio stations not to broadcast the names of casualties. This is deeply appreciated as broadcast of casualty lists would, in effect, set up obituary columns on the air when such time can be used to elevate morale rather than depress it. Because of opportunity for mispronunciation of names it is felt that such lists should appear in print rather than uttered over the air. No objection to mentioning, however, occasional newsworthy names or, of course, broadcast of numbers of casualties.'

Signed: Ed Kirby, Chief,
Radio Branch, War Department.

WATCH REQUESTS CAREFULLY

Whenever a station receives a request, ostensibly originating with one of the branches of the armed forces, to make an announcement of any kind be sure to authenticate it. Broadcasters are cautioned not to put any announcements on air notifying military or naval personnel to return to posts or stations unless they are absolutely certain that the person requesting the announcement has proper authority.

HELP RECRUITING

Manpower is our first need right now. Army, navy and marines have asked for more recruiting help. Suggestions for your help will be outlined in letters mailed this week.

NATIONAL ASSOCIATION OF BROADCASTER WARTIME GUIDE

The following is the text of the National Association of
Broadcasters Wartime Guide, issued to American radio
stations on 18 December 1941:*

    This is a different war. It affects all phases of
the nation's activity and reaches into every home. This is
total war and victory requires the combined effort of all
our people. While we have learned much, from broadcasting
war news since 1939, we now have new responsibilities and
new opportunities. The relationship between broadcasting
and government and the manner in which it will perform its
function as the chief source of news and information
requires careful appraisal. Upon the judgments and
policies now formulated will depend our effectiveness.
    The broad outlines of the policies to be followed
in dealing with news and radio were given by the President
in his speech of December 9.
    The National Association of Broadcasters after
careful consultation with the military branches of the
government as well as other agencies has attempted to make
more detailed and specific the broader principles as
enunciated by the President. With the objective of setting
forth certain basic requirements your Association offers to
broadcasters this pamphlet of recommendations as a guide to
wartime broadcasters.
    In general, accept the fact that this is likely to
be a long war--with both reverses and triumphs. Avoid
broadcasting the news in a manner that is likely to cause
exaggerated optimism. Likewise avoid creating an
atmosphere of defeatism and despair. At all times practice
moderation in writing, delivering and scheduling
broadcasts.
    The writing should avoid sensationalism.
    The delivery should be calm, accurate, factual.
    There should be a minimum of production trappings
surrounding news broadcasts. The news of America at war is
sufficiently exciting; do not try to make it more so by

---

*Quoted in Robert E. Summers, ed., *Wartime Censorship
of Press and Radio* (New York: H. W. Wilson, 1942), pp. 283-
85.

presenting it with sound-effects. The tension needs to be
lessened, not increased.

Newscasts should be scheduled at regular intervals,
and, in the absence of news of extreme importance, this
regular schedule should be followed.

Artificial efforts to stimulate listening audience
by promises of immediate interruption of regular programs
for important news broadcasts should not be attempted. Let
the events speak for themselves.

Extreme care should be used in the handling and
broadcast of any communiques or radio reports from our
enemies.

They should not be used unless coupled, by careful
editing, with known facts or an official statement on the
same subject by our government. If you don't have the
facts or an official statement on the same subject, don't
broadcast the enemy communique until you get them.
In this connection, broadcasters should remember that
extraordinary care must be taken to insure that those who
tune in late do not get a wrong impression. Remember the
Men from Mars!

Remember we are at war with other Axis countries as
well as Japan. Their communiques should be considered in
the same light as those of the Japs.

The broadcasting industry has been given to
understand that it can use news from recognized press
services because responsibility for that news rests with
the press services. News gathered from other sources must
be thoroughly checked and verified before broadcasting.

Do not broadcast rumors, 'hot tips,' or
'unconfirmed reports,' no matter what their source. 'Hot
tips' and rumors may burn your fingers.

If you have the slightest doubt on any story, check
with your press association. It is better to have no news
than to broadcast false or harmful news.

In this connection, a word of caution on news
flashes. A good practice is to wait a few minutes after
the first flash until you are perfectly satisfied from the
following story that the flash is borne out. Radio's speed
of light is cause for caution.

Do not broadcast news which concerns war production
figures unless such news is officially released by the
government.

Do not broadcast the movement of naval or any other
vessels.

Do not broadcast news about the movement of troops
or personnel either outside or with'n the continental
limits, unless it has been released officially by the War
or Navy Departments.

Do not broadcast the location of vessels, either
under construction or about to be launched.

Do not broadcast figures of Selective Service enrollments and inductions.

Do not broadcast personal observations on weather conditions. Watch sports broadcasts for this. A late night or early morning comment that 'it's a fine, clear night (or morning)' might be invaluable information to the enemy. Stick to official weather reports you station receives from your local weather bureau.

Do not broadcast such imperatives as 'Attention all men! Report to your local Civil Defense headquarters tonight at eight.' Announcements may be requested in that manner. They should be changed to qualify the source at the beginning, such as: 'The local Civil Defense Committee requests all men, etc.' Reserve such 'attention compellers' for important war purposes.

Do not overestimate American power nor underestimate the enemy strength and thereby tend to create complacent confidence. Stick to the facts as presented in official releases.

Do not allow sponsors to use the news as a springboard for commercials. Such practices as starting commercials with 'Now some good news, etc.' should never be permitted. Also it is important that such news-phrases ass 'Bulletin,' 'Flash,' 'News' and the like be used only in their legitimate functions. Do not permit,'Here's good news! The Bargain Basement announces drastic reductions, etc.'

Do not use any sound-effects on dramatic programs, commercial announcements or otherwise which might be confused by the listener with air raid alarms, alert signals, etc.

Do not try to second-guess or master-mind our military officials. Leave this for established military analysts and experts, who are experienced enough to await the facts before drawing conclusions.

Do not broadcast any long list of casualties. This has been specifically forbidden.

Do not permit speakers, in discussions of controversial public issues, to say anything of aid to the enemy.

Do not broadcast the location of plants engaged in the manufacture of war materials unless approved by the government. This applies to emergencies such as explosions, sabotage, etc., unless such reports have been approved by government or cleared at the source by press associations.

Do not take chances with ad lib broadcasts, on the street or in the studio. An open microphone accessible to the general public constitutes a very real hazard in times of war. Questions should be prepared in advance, and extreme care should be exercised to avoid the asking of questions which would draw out any information of value to the enemy. Any questions regarding the war or war production might make trouble.

Do--Maintain constant vigil over the news machines. Be sure to designate a responsible staff member in charge of the news at all hours of your operation. That person should be the one to determine the advisability of breaking programs for news bulletins, flashes, etc., and should be responsible for all news during the period he is designated in charge of the news machines.

Look for further instructions on the press wires, from the National Association of Broadcasters, the War Department, the Navy, or other official sources.

See that every member of your staff knows and understands these guides. Let your entire news staff and announcers know your policy.

File a complete script of all your news broadcasts. Keep the file until the war ends.

Prepare and present your news factually, authentically, calmly. This is repetition, but this caution cannot be repeated too much.

Do your job as best you can, knowing it is one of the significant jobs in this all-out war in which America is engaged. Do your job measured to even stricter standards that we have set. Do your job in a manner that will satisfy yourself, advance the cause of free radio and serve the best interests of your country.

APPENDIX 3

APPENDIX 3

U.S. MILITARY ASSISTANCE COMMAND, VIETNAM
PRESS GROUND RULES

Rules Governing Public Release of Military
Information in Vietnam (Effective 1 November 1966)

The following is the text of press ground rules issued 31
October 1966:*

BACKGROUND

The basic principle governing the public release of
military information in Vietnam is that the maximum amount
of information will be made available, consistent with the
requirement for security.

In past wars a great deal of information could be, and
was, denied the enemy on the basis that he did not have
ready access to it. This is not the case in Vietnam. By
their very nature, subversion and guerrilla warfare make it
impossible to safeguard many types of information that once
were carefully protected. Thus, the arrival of a major US
unit is announced immediately, rather than weeks or even
months later. Pinpoint datelines are permitted. In-
country strength figures, by service, are released at
regular intervals. Casualty figures are release weekly.

In Vietnam the greatest problem in achieving a full
flow of information to newsmen and thence to the public is
not that of deciding whether the information is releasable,
but that of physically gathering, transmitting and checking
information from widely scattered locations linked together

---

*As quoted in U.S. Military Assistance Command,
Vietnam, *Public Information Policies and Procedures*
(Military Assistance Command-Vietnam Directive 360-1),
Saigon, 1967, Annex A.

only be air transportation and an almost saturated communications system.

In the past, certain ground rules have defined the items of information that are not releasable and those that are releasable. The ground rules have been reviewed to insure that they are clearly stated, that they are limited to those required to preserve military security and that the principle of making the maximum amount of information available to the public is being followed.

The situation in South Vietnam is such that correspondents may come into possession of information which has not been released officially under the ground rules set forth herein. Such information is not to be transmitted or released to the public until officially released by American or other Free World spokesmen in regard to their respective national forces. Official Government of Vietnam (GVN) and U.S. Military Assistance Command, Vietnam (MACV) accreditation is issued on this condition. Deliberate violation of these conditions or ground rules by a correspondent will be regarded as a basis for suspension or cancellation of accreditation.

Correspondents may find that, at times, their movements may be restricted to certain tactical areas. These restrictions are kept to a minimum but they may be applied by a commanding officer when in his opinion the nature of operation warrants such action. Correspondents will be advised of such restrictions by the commanding officer of the unit or by the Information Officer representative of the headquarters involved, or by the unit G2/S2 if there is no information officer representative present.

GROUND RULES

1. The Commander, United States Military Assistance Command, Vietnam is the sole releasing authority for all information material, including photography, pertaining to US military activities in Vietnam and gathered or produced by military individuals or organizations. Local commanders are delegated the authority to release hometown news material. As authorized by COMUSMACV, the Chief of Information or his duty appointed representative is the official MACV military spokesman.

2. Information cleared for release will be made available to the press by MACV through one or more of the following means.

    a. Daily press release.

b. Daily press briefing.

c. Call outs.

d. Special press handouts.

3. Releasable Information.

a. General.

(1) Arrival of major units in country when officially announced by COMUSMACV.

(2) Strength figures of US forces, by service, when announced by COMUSMACV.

(3) Official total casualty figures on a weekly and cumulative basis, as furnished by Department of Defense on the basis of reports from the services.

(4) Enemy casualty figures for each action or operation, daily and cumulatively.

b. Ground/Naval Operations.

(1) Casualties suffered by friendly units in an announced operation in terms of 'light,' 'moderate' or 'heavy' as applied to the size of the force in that action or operation.

(2) Size of friendly forces involved in an action or operation using general terms such as 'multibattalion.'

(3) Information regarding details of a tactical operation when release has been authorized by COMUSMACV (see paragraph 1, General Notes).

c. Air Operations.

(1) Target or targets hit, to included general location and category of target.

(2) Identification as to whether it was VNAF, US or a joint VNAF/US strike.

(3) Whether aircraft were land-based or carrier-based. Names of carriers when their aircraft are involved.

(4) Time of the attack in general terms.

(5) General evaluation of success of the mission.

(6) Types of ordnance expended in general terms, such as 250-pound fragmentation bombs, 500-pound general purpose bombs, rockets, .50 caliber ammunition, 20mm cannon fire.

(7) Number of missions over North Vietnam; number of sorties over the Republic of Vietnam (RVN).

(8) Types of aircraft involved.

(9) Weather enroute and over the target during a strike.

(10) Pilot sightings of unfriendly aircraft.

(11) Periodically, the number of aircraft downed:

(a) By hostile fire in South Vietnam.

(b) By hostile fire in North Vietnam.

(12) Volume of enemy antiaircraft fire in general terms.

4. Information not releasable under any circumstances.

a. General.

(1) Future plans, operations, or strikes.

(2) Information on or confirmation of Rules of Engagement.

(3) Amounts of ordnance and fuel moved by support units or on hand in combat units.

b. Ground/Naval Operations.

(1) Exact number and type or identification of casualties suffered by friendly units.

(2) During an operation, unit designations and troop movements, tactical deployments, name of operation and size of friendly forces involved, until officially released by MACV.

(3) Intelligence unit activities, methods of operation, or specific location.

c. Air Operations.

(1) The number of sorties and the amount of ordnance expended on strikes outside the RVN.

(2) Information on aircraft taking off for strikes, enroute to, or returning from target area. Information on strikes while they are in progress.

(3) Identity of units and locations of air bases from which aircraft are launched on combat operations.

(4) Number of aircraft damaged or any other indicator of effectiveness of ground antiaircraft defenses.

(5) Tactical specifics, such as altitudes, courses, speeds, or angle of attack. (General terms such as 'low and fast' may be used.)

(6) Information on or confirmation regarding strikes which do not take place for any reason, including bad weather.

(7) Specific identification of enemy weapon system utilized to down friendly aircraft.

(8) Details concerning downed aircraft while SAR operations are in progress.

GENERAL NOTES

1. The initial release of information pertaining to any tactical operation in the field will be made by the MACV Office of Information (MACOI) when, in the opinion of the field force commander concerned, the release of such information will not adversely affect the security of his command. This condition will exist when it can be presumed that the enemy is aware of the general strength and location of the friendly force(s), and may occur either before or after there has been significant contact. The field force commander's recommendation for release does not constitute authority for commanders subordinate to MACV to effect release to news media. Initial announcement of an operation will be made only by MACOI.

2.   Casualty information, as it relates to the
notification of the next of kin, is extremely sensitive.
By Executive direction, next of kin of all military
fatalities must be notified in person by an officer of the
appropriate service.   There have been instances in which
next of kin have learned of the death or wounding of a
loved one through news media.   The problem is particularly
difficult for visual media.   Casualty photographs can show
a recognizable face, name tag, jewelry or other identifying
feature or item.   The anguish that sudden recognition at
home can cause is out of proportion to the news value of
the photograph or film.   Although the casualty reporting
and notification system works on a priority basis,
correspondents are urged to keep this problem in mind when
covering an action in the field.   Names of casualties whose
next of kin have been notified can be verified by the MACV
Information Office and by the Directorate of News Services
in the Office of the Assistant Secretary of Defense (Public
Affairs).

3.   Only two Viet Cong casualty figures are release -
'killed in action' and 'captured.'   There is no way to get
a 'wounded' figure although there are indications that for
every Viet Cong killed, one and one-half VC are wounded
seriously enough to require hospital treatment.   The
'captured' figure may be broken down to 'Viet Cong' and
'Viet Cong Suspects.'   The total is a firm figure.   Any
'Viet Cong Killed' figure released by MACV will have been
verified on the scene by US military personnel to the
extent permitted by the military situation.   It cannot be
an exact figure, but it is probable that duplications and
other errors on the high side are more than offset by the
number of Viet Cong dead who are carried away or buried
nearby, by those who subsequently die of wounds or by those
killed by artillery concentrations and air strikes not
followed up by ground action.   Thus, when the briefer
announces a specific number of Viet Cong killed in a
particular operation or over a given period, that figure is
not as precise as the popular term 'body count' would
imply.   Neither is it a guess or loose estimate.   It is the
best figure that can be developed and, as noted, probably
is conservative in the long run.

4.   Members of the Military Assistance Command
Information Office are available to discuss any questions
which may arise concerning the release of military
information.

5.   Requests for information concerning nonmilitary
activities and Republic of Vietnam military activities
should be addressed to the Government of Vietnam, the

Republic of Vietnam Armed Forces, the US Mission or the Public Information representative of the appropriate Free World Force or activity.

6. Whenever possible, changes to this memorandum will be brought to the attention of correspondents before they are put into effect.

Nguyen Bao Tri
Major General, Army of the Republic of Vietnam
Minister of Information & Open Arms
Government of Vietnam   _____SIGNED_____

Barry Zorthian
Minister Counselor for Information
US Mission, Vietnam   _____SIGNED_____

Rodger R. Bankston
Colonel, US Army
Chief of Information, MACV   _____SIGNED_____

<u>U.S. Military Assistance Command, Vietnam</u>
<u>March 1968 Interpretation of Ground Rules Memorandum</u>*

<u>MEMORANDUM FOR THE PRESS</u>   27 March 1968

Subject: Interpretation of Ground Rules

1.   A MACOI memorandum to the press of 29 January 1968
reminded all press members of the ground rules involving
ground combat to which they agreed when they were
accredited to MACV.   A follow-up memorandum of 26 February
further explained one of the rules.

2.   Members of the press have been most cooperative in
attempting to stem the flow of important intelligence
information to the enemy.   However based both on logic and
the many queries received from newsmen, it is obvious that
no set of ground rules can cover every tactical situation
encountered by newsmen in the field.   Although relatively
few in number, the 'gray areas' cannot be eliminated.

3.   To assist newsmen in correctly interpreting any ground
rule gray areas, MACV will provide 24-hour service to
anyone who obtains information which he feels is subject to
interpretation under the ground rules.   Any newsman in the
I CTZ (I Corps Tactical Zone) who is concerned about the
intelligence value of material he wishes to use in a story
should contact the ISO at the MACV Press Center, Da Nang:
phone Da Nang 6259.   Elsewhere in Vietnam, queries should
be addressed to MACV extensions 3163 or 3989 where someone
able to make a decision will always be on duty.

4.   We hope that this service will help ensure a maximum
flow of information while insuring the necessary protection
of our troops.

5.   For your information, a copy of the key ground rules is
attached.

---

*As quoted in U.S. Army War College Strategic Studies
Institute, 'Press Coverage of the Vietnam War: The Third
View,' Unpublished Study Group Report, U.S. Army War
College, Carlisle Barracks, Pa., 1979, p. C-1.

                                    --*SIGNED*--
                                    WINANT SIDLE
                                    Brigadier General, USA
                                    Chief of Information

1 INCL
as

Excerpts from 'Rules Governing Public Release of Military Information' (31 October 1966 & 29 March 1967)

The following information is <u>not</u> releasable, unless and until released by MACV.

1.   Future plans, operations or strikes.
2.   Information on or confirmation of Rules of Engagement.
3.   Amounts of ordnance and fuel moved by support units or on hand in combat units (ordnance includes weapons or weapons systems).
4.   During an operation, unit designations and troop movements, tactical deployments, name of operation and size of friendly forces involved.
5.   Intelligence unit activities, methods of operation, or specific locations.
6.   Exact number and type of casualties or damage suffered by friendly units.
7.   Number of sorties and the amount of ordnance expended on strikes outside of RVN.
8.   Information on aircraft taking off for strikes, enroute to, or returning from target areas. Information on strikes while they are in progress.
9.   Identity of units and locations of air bases from which aircraft are launched on combat operations.
10.   Number of aircraft damaged or any other indicator of effectiveness or ineffectiveness of ground antiaircraft defenses.
11.   Tactical specifics, such as altitudes, course, speeds, or angle of attack. (General descriptions such as 'low and fast' may be used.)
12.   Information on or confirmation of planned strikes which do not take place for any reason, including bad weather.
13.   Specific identification of enemy weapons systems utilized to down friendly aircraft.
14.   Details concerning downed aircraft while SAR operations are in progress.
15.   Aerial photos of fixed installations.

-END-

APPENDIX 4

APPENDIX 4

U.S. DEPARTMENT OF DEFENSE DIRECTIVE
WARTIME INFORMATION SECURITY PROGRAM

Department of Defense Directives System Transmittal

May 21, 1971
DoD Directive 5230.7, June 25, 1965.

REPRINT

The attached reprint of Department of Defense Directive
5230.7, "Wartime Information Security Program (WISP),"
dated June 25, 1965, incorporates current authorized
changes, which are indicated by marginal asterisks.
Previous changes to pages 1, 4, 11, 12 and 15 have been
incorporated.

The attached reprint changes the program title from
"Censorship Planning" to "Wartime Information Security
Program (WISP)" wherever it appears throughout the
Directive.

The reprinted Directive should be substituted for copies of
5230.7 and Changes 1 and 2 previously distributed.

EFFECTIVE DATE AND IMPLEMENTATION

This change is effective immediately. At the direction of
DoD Components, changes in existing regulations may be
postponed until such time as a substantive change is made
to the Directive.

--SIGNED--
MAURICE W. ROCHE
Director, Correspondence and Directives Division
OASD(Administration)

DEPARTMENT OF DEFENSE DIRECTIVE

SUBJECT: Wartime Information Security Program (WISP)

References:
    (a) DoD Directive 5230.7 'Censorship Planning', May 29, 1959 (hereby cancelled)
    (b) DoD Directive 5120.33, 'Classification Management Program,' January 8, 1963
    (c) National Censorship Agreement Between the Department of Defense and the Office of Emergency Planning, October 1, 1963

I. REISSUANCE

This Directive reissues policy on, and assigns responsibility for, WISP planning involving the Department of Defense. Reference (a) is hereby cancelled.

II. APPLICABILITY AND SCOPE

This Directive applies to the Military Departments, the Organization of the Joint Chiefs of Staff, and the Assistant Secretaries of Defense (Administration) and (Public Affairs), and governs planning within the DoD for National WISP including Armed Forces, Civil, Enemy Prisoner of War and Civilian Internee, and Field Press WISP.

III. DEFINITIONS

A. <u>WISP</u>. The control and examination of communications to prevent disclosure of information of value to an enemy, and to collect information of value to the United States.

B. <u>United States</u>. The term 'United States' includes the fifty states, the Commonwealth of Puerto Rico, Guam, the Virgin Islands, American Samoa and Swain's Island, the Canal Zone, the Trust Territories of the Pacific Islands, and any territory or area under the jurisdiction of the United States, or which is committed to its control as administering authority by treaty or international agreement.

C.   <u>Communication</u>. The term `communication`
     includes any letter, book, plan, map, or other
     paper, picture, sound recording, or other
     reproduction, telegram, cablegram, wireless
     message, or conversation transmitted over wire,
     radio, television, optical, or other electro-
     magnetic system, and any message transmitted by
     any signalling device or any other means.

D.   <u>National WISP</u>. The control and examination of
     communications entering, leaving, transiting,
     or touching the borders of the United States,
     and the voluntary withholding from publication
     by the domestic public media industries of
     military and other information which should not
     be released in the interest of the safety and
     defense of the United States and it Allies.

     1.   <u>National Communications WISP</u>. - Within the
          scope of National WISP, the control and
          examination of communications transmitted
          or received over the circuits of commercial
          communications companies classified by the
          Federal Communications Commission as
          `common carriers,` and not under the
          control, use, supervision, or inspection of
          a Federal agency.

     2.   <u>National Postal and Travelers WISP</u>. -
          Within the scope of National WISP, the
          control and examination of postal
          communications, communications carried on
          the person or in the baggage or personal
          possessions of travelers, and all other
          communications subject to review and not
          within the purview of other elements of
          National WISP.

E.   <u>Armed Forces WISP</u>. The examination and control
     of personal communications to or from persons
     in the Armed Forces of the United States and
     persons accompanying or serving with the Armed
     Forces of the United States.

F.   <u>Civil WISP</u>. Review of civilian communications,
     such as messages, printed matter, and films,
     entering, leaving, or circulating within areas
     or territories occupied or controlled by the
     Armed Forces of the United States.

G. **Enemy Prisoner of War and Civilian Internee
    WISP**. The review of communications to and from
    enemy Prisoners of War and civilian internees
    held by the United States Armed Forces.

H. **Field Press WISP**. The security review of news
    material subject to the jurisdiction of the
    Armed Forces of the United States, including
    all information or material intended for
    dissemination to the public.

I. **Primary WISP**. Armed Forces review performed by
    personnel of a company, battery, squadron,
    ship, station, base, or similar unit, on the
    personal communications of persons assigned,
    attached, or otherwise under the jurisdiction
    of a unit.

J. **Secondary WISP**. Armed Forces review performed
    on the personal communications of officers,
    civilian employees, and accompanying civilians
    of the Armed Forces of the United States, and
    on those personal communications of enlisted
    personnel of the armed forces not subject to
    Armed Forces primary review, or those requiring
    reexamination.

IV. **NATIONAL WISP**

A. **Objectives**. The objectives of National WISP
    are to (1) deny to the enemy information which
    would aid his war effort or would hinder our
    own; and (2) collect information of value in
    prosecuting the war and make it available to
    proper authorities.

B. **Assumptions**.

    1. In the event of war, the President will
        impose National WISP.

    2. The imposition of National WISP will be
        supported by appropriate legislation.

    3. Upon implementation of National WISP, the
        President will establish an Office of WISP
        and appoint a Director of WISP.

    4. The Office of WISP will be an independent
        Federal Agency reporting directly to the
        President.

C. <u>National WISP Operating and Planning Principles</u>

1. WISP is an indispensable part of war, and
    planning for it should keep pace with other
    war plans.

2. WISP restraints will be enforced only for
    reasons of military import as described in
    subsection IV.A, above. WISP will <u>not</u> be
    used to (a) suppress information, other
    than in the interest of national security
    or defense, (b) assist in the enforcement
    of peacetime statutes unconnected with the
    war effort, or (c) act as a guardian of
    public morals.

3. Although there are no restrictions on the
    authority of the Director of WISP (to be
    established by the President in accordance
    with paragraph IV.B.3, above), National
    WISP normally will not be exercised over
    Government communications, over non-
    government communications facilities
    allocated to Federal agencies, or those
    which may come under the control, use,
    supervision, or inspection of Federal
    agencies.

4. During the interim between imposition of
    National WISP by the President and the
    determination by the Director of WISP that
    the Office of WISP is prepared to assume
    control of Postal and Travelers WISP,
    Telecommunications WISP, and the Special
    Analysis Division, the Secretary of Defense
    will be responsible for such functions.

5. The Director of WISP will notify the
    Secretary of Defense when the Office of
    WISP is prepared to assume control of the
    functions set forth in paragraph IV.C.4,
    above, after which date responsibility for
    such functions shall be vested in the
    Director of WISP.

6. After the Director of WISP assumes control
    of Postal and Travelers WISP,
    Telecommunications WISP, and the Special
    Analysis Division, military personnel of
    the DoD assigned to the Office of WISP will

be under the administrative control of their Services, and the operational control of the Director of WISP. Military personnel may be withdrawn by their respective Services as mutually agreed upon by the Secretary of Defense and the Director of WISP.

7. At the time of transfer of control from the Department of Defense to the Office of WISP, all items of equipment and supplies necessary for and being used or allocated to WISP operations, and all leases that have been entered into for WISP operations, will be transferred to the Director of WISP without reimbursement.

D. <u>Delineation of Planning Responsibilities</u>. Responsibilities for advance National WISP planning are assigned as follows:

1. The Office of Emergency Preparedness (OEP), under the provisions of reference (c), will:

    a. Coordinate and monitor all aspects of National WISP planning.

    b. Develop a plan for establishing Public Media WISP.

    c. Develop a plan, in coordination with the DoD and other interested agencies, for establishing an Office of WISP.

    d. Furnish policy and training guidance, a coordinator, and training space for the Special Analysis Division, Office of WISP.

    e. Develop plans for the Office of WISP providing for the coordination of the procurement of equipment necessary to support the operations of the Special Analysis Division.

    f. Accept responsibility for procuring space for all elements of National Headquarters of the Office of WISP.

g. Develop plans for the Office of WISP to coordinate the hiring of all civilian personnel to be used by all elements of the National Headquarters of the Office of WISP.

h. Maintain an activation file containing the necessary directives for the establishment of National WISP. This includes proposed proclamations, executive orders and legislation.

i. Coordinate, with foreign governments, in conjunction with the DoD, liaison on National WISP policy matters.

2. The Department of Defense under the provisions of reference (c) will:

a. Develop plans and preparations for National Postal and Travelers WISP, National Telecommunications WISP, and the Special Analysis Division as elements of the Office of WISP.

b. Maintain liaison with foreign governments on technical and operational planning matters.

c. Maintain duplicate activation files containing the necessary directives for the establishment of National WISP.

d. Achieve and maintain an adequate degree of readiness at all times for the activation of those elements of the Office of WISP for which the DoD is responsible.

E. Specific Responsibilities Within the Department of Defense

1. The Assistant Secretary of Defense (Administration) is responsible for:

a. Over-all coordination and direction of the National WISP policy and program within the DoD.

b. Representing the DoD with other

government agencies on National WISP
matters.

c. Maintaining liaison with foreign
    governments on National WISP matters.

d. Maintaining activation files containing
    necessary directives, proposed
    proclamations, executive orders, and
    legislation. Those will be duplicates
    of activation files maintained in the
    Office of Emergency Preparedness.

e. Monitoring the Military Departments'
    National WISP functions and
    responsibilities to achieve and
    maintain readiness for the imposition
    of National Postal and Travelers WISP,
    National Telecommunications WISP and
    the operation of the Special Analysis
    Division.

2. The Assistant Secretary of Defense (Public
    Affairs) is responsible for:

    a. Over-all coordination and direction
        within the DoD for National Public
        Media WISP policy and program.

    b. Representing the DoD with other
        government agencies on National Public
        Media WISP matters and for developing a
        policy and program covering DoD
        participation in National Public Media
        WISP.

3. The Secretary of the Army, in coordination
    with the Secretary of the Air Force, is
    responsible for development of plans and
    preparations for Postal and Travelers WISP
    as an element of National WISP. These
    responsibilities include:

    a. Preparing logistic and operation plans
        for Postal and Travelers WISP.

    b. Preparing operational instructions and
        guidance for review.

    c. Developing plans for M-day recruitment
        and assignment of qualified civilians

to selected positions in Postal and Travelers WISP.

    d.   Maintaining liaison with other government agencies on planning and activation matters.

4.   The Secretary of the Army is responsible for developing and preparing plans for the Special Analysis Division as an element of National WISP, and for planning for and operating the National Postal and Travelers WISP organization and the Special Analysis Division, when so directed. This responsibility includes:

    a.   Selecting and training personnel of the Reserve Components of the Department of the Army for mobilization assignment to National Postal and Travelers WISP.

    b.   Selecting personnel of the Reserve Components of the Department of the Army for mobilization assignment to the Army Element, Special Analysis Division.

    c.   Developing Tables of Distribution for M-day recruitment and assignment of civilians to positions in Postal and Travelers WISP.

    d.   Stockpiling essential supplies and equipment as a readiness measure for National Postal and Travelers WISP.

5.   The Secretary of the Navy is responsible for developing plans and preparing for activation of, and the operation of, Telecommunications WISP as an element of National WISP. This responsibility includes:

    a.   Preparing logistic and operations plans for National Telecommunications WISP.

    b.   Recruiting and assigning personnel of the Reserve Components of the Department of the Navy to mobilization billets in Telecommunications WISP.

c. Selecting personnel of the Reserve
Components of the Department of the
Navy for mobilization assignment to the
Navy Element, Special Analysis
Division.

d. Developing plans for immediate M-day
recruitment and assignment of qualified
civilians to selected positions in
National Telecommunications WISP.

e. Conducting liaison with commercial
communications companies, governmental
agencies, and others as required on
technical operational planning and
activation matters.

f. Developing and administering necessary
training in Telecommunications WISP
including the conduct of seminars and
exercises, and preparation of curricula
and guidance for review units.

g. Preparing and promulgating operational
procedure and guidance for reviewers.

h. Stockpiling certain essential supplies
and equipment as a readiness measure
for National Telecommunications WISP.

6. The Secretary of the Air Force is
responsible for making the following
preparations and plans for Postal and
Travelers WISP and the Special Analysis
Division as elements of National WISP.
This responsibility includes:

a. Selecting personnel of the Reserve
Components of the Department of the Air
Force for mobilization assignment to
National Postal and Travelers WISP.

b. Selecting personnel of the Reserve
Components of the Department of the Air
Force for mobilization assignment to
the Air Force Element, Special Analysis
Division.

c. Training personnel of the Reserve
Components of the Department of the Air
Force and making such personnel

available to the Department of the Army for duty upon imposition of National WISP.

F. National WISP Planning Security Classification

   1. The fact of the existence of National WISP planning is unclassified.

   2. Classification will be determined in accordance with issuances under reference (b).

V. FIELD PRESS WISP

A. Objectives and Scope

   1. The objectives of Field Press WISP are to (a) insure the prompt release to the public of the maximum information consistent with security, and (b) prevent the disclosure of information which could assist the enemy.

   2. Accreditation of correspondents, provisions of communication facilities, civil review, and the internal dissemination of communications are not within the province of field press WISP.

B. Policy

   1. The governing principle will be that security review of news material will be accomplished within the shortest practicable time, and the maximum information released to the public consistent without being of aid to the enemy.

   2. Every effort will be made to conduct field press review at locations convenient to processing and transmission facilities.

   3. Field press review will be conducted in accordance with United States Armed Forces doctrine which will apply to the security review of news material subject to the jurisdiction of elements of the Armed Forces, whether acting jointly or independently. The security review of news material subject to the jurisdiction of the

United States Armed Forces portion of combined commands will be governed by procedures prescribed by the combined force commander insofar as such procedure is in consonance with the principles set forth in paragraphs V.B.1 and 2., above.

4. Upon declaration of war, or if the United States is attacked, or if the United States is believed about to be attacked, field press WISP may be established in the United States by the Secretary of Defense with the approval of the President.

5. Field press WISP may be placed into effect immediately outside the Continental United States by a joint, specified or other area commander of an area in which United States Armed Forces are operating, in the event of (a) a declaration of war by the United States, (b) an armed attack upon the United States, its territories or possessions, or an area occupied or controlled by the United States, (c) an armed attack on the Armed Forces of the United States, or (d) the commitment to combat of the Armed Forces of the United States as a separate force or as a part of a United Nations effort.

6. Wherever initiated or established, Field Press WISP will cease only upon direction of the Secretary of Defense.

C. Responsibilities

1. The Assistant Secretary of Defense (Public Affairs) will develop over-all plans and provide policy direction for the operation of field press WISP.

2. The Secretaries of the Military Departments will be responsible for:

a. Preparing logistic and operations plans for Field Press WISP .

b. Selecting and training personnel for assignment to Field Press WISP .

        c. Preparing and issuing uniform technical
            operational instructions and guidance
            to reviewers.

        d. Stockpiling essential supplies for
            Field Press WISP.

VI.   ARMED FORCES WISP

      A. Objectives. The objectives of Armed Forces
          WISP are to (1) prevent the disclosure of
          information which might assist the enemy or
          which might adversely affect any policy of the
          United States; and (2) collect and disseminate
          information which might assist the United
          States in the successful prosecution of a war.

      B. Policy

          1. Armed Forces WISP may be imposed in time of
              peace only when specifically directed by
              (a) the President, (b) the Secretary of
              Defense, or (c) by the commander of a
              unified or specified command, as an
              emergency security measure, upon
              indications that an outbreak of hostilities
              is imminent or has occurred within his
              area.

          2, Subsequent to a declaration of war by the
              United States, the following conditions
              will govern the imposition of Armed Forces
              WISP.

              a. Within the Continental United States

                  (1) If the United States is attacked
                       or believed about to be attacked,
                       Armed Forces WISP will be
                       established under military control
                       by order of the Secretary of
                       Defense.

                  (2) When deemed necessary to maintain
                       security at installations under
                       military control, Armed Forces
                       WISP may be imposed after approval
                       by the Secretary of Defense. The
                       appropriate Military Department
                       will request such approval.

(3)   Responsible commanders will impose
      immediate review at ports of water
      or aerial embarkation and related
      staging areas to maintain adequate
      security, and advise the
      Department of the Army, Navy, or
      the Air Force, as appropriate, of
      such imposition.

b.   Outside the Continental United States.
     In all land or water areas where
     persons in, serving with, or
     accompanying, the Armed Forces of the
     United States are stationed, Armed
     Forces WISP will be imposed
     immediately.

3.   Secondary Armed Forces WISP will be
     performed by the military components as
     directed by the appropriate unified or
     specified commanders in compliance with the
     order imposing Armed Forces WISP.

4.   Armed Forces WISP will cease only when so
     directed by the Secretary of Defense upon
     recommendation by the Joint Staff of the
     appropriate Military Department.

C.   Responsibilities

1.   The Secretaries of the Military Departments
     will be responsible for:

     a.   Preparing over-all plans and uniform
          policies for their support of Armed
          Forces WISP.

     b.   Preparing logistic and operations plans
          for Armed Forces WISP.

     c.   Selecting and training personnel for
          assignment to Armed Forces WISP.

     d.   Preparing and issuing Armed Forces WISP
          regulations.

     e.   Stockpiling essential supplies for
          Armed Forces WISP.

VIII.   CIVIL WISP

A. Objectives. The objectives of Civil WISP are
    to (1) collect and disseminate information
    which might assist the United States in the
    successful prosecution of a war, and (2)
    prevent the disclosure of information which
    might assist the enemy, or which might
    adversely affect any policy of the United
    States.

B. Policy

    1. When Civil WISP is established in a foreign
        territory, jurisdiction will be exercised
        over all communications entering, leaving,
        or circulating within the territory, except
        those controlled by other forms of United
        States or Allied WISP.

        a. Establishment of Civil WISP in a
            foreign territory controlled by the
            Armed Forces of the United States may
            be directed by the Secretary of
            Defense.

        b. Establishment of Civil WISP in foreign
            territories occupied by the Armed
            Forces of the United States as the
            result of military operations may be
            directed by the appropriate unified or
            specified commander.

    2. The Secretary of Defense will determine the
        time and phasing of Civil WISP termination
        or transfer to other than military control.

C. Responsibilities

    1. The Secretary of the Army is responsible
        for the continuous planning for Civil WISP
        as a military measure, working in close
        cooperation with the Secretaries of the
        Navy and Air Force in:

        a. Preparing logistical and operational
            plans.

        b. Planning for the selection and training
            of military personnel for Civil WISP
            duty assignments.

c. Conducting operational planning and
       activation liaison with other Federal
       agencies.

   d. Preparing and issuing technical
       operational instructions and guidance
       for reviewers.

   e. Monitoring the conduct of Civil WISP
       when imposed.

2. The Secretary of the Navy will assist the
   Secretary of the Army in developing plans,
   policy, and preparations for the
   telecommunications element of Civil WISP,
   including the selection, training and
   assignment of Naval personnel to Civil
   WISP.

3. THe Secretary of the Air Force will assist
   the Secretary of the Army in developing
   plans, policy, and preparations for the
   Postal and Travelers element of Civil WISP,
   including the selection, training and
   assignment of Air Force personnel to Civil
   WISP.

4. Unified and specified commanders will
   operate Civil WISP as a military measure in
   United States occupied territory, or in
   controlled territory within limits
   determined by mutual agreement between the
   recognized government of the controlled
   territory and the United States Government.

5. Unified and specified commanders will plan
   for the operation of Civil WISP in areas
   subject to occupation of control in
   accordance with war plans.

VIII. **ENEMY PRISONER OF WAR WISP**

   A. **Objectives**

   1. To collect and disseminate information that
      will assist the United States in the
      successful prosecution of a war.

   2. To prevent the disclosure of information
      which might assist the enemy, or which

might affect any policy of the United States.

3. To collect and furnish to authorities of enemy prisoner of war and civilian internee camps information that may help maintain discipline and physical security.

B. Policy

1. The operation of Enemy Prisoner of War and Civilian Internee WISP will be undertaken only with a full understanding of the rights guaranteed to enemy prisoners of war and civilian internees by the Geneva Conventions to which the United States is a signatory.

2. All enemy prisoner of war and civilian internee mail, with the exceptions required by the Geneva Conventions, will be subject to review.

C. Responsibilities

1. The Secretary of the Army is responsible for continuous planning for Enemy Prisoner of War and Civilian Internee WISP and will exercise the following responsibilities in close cooperation with the Secretary of the Navy and the Secretary of the Air Force:

a. Pre-mobilization planning for Enemy Prisoner of War and Civilian Internee WISP.

b. Preparation and promulgation of Enemy Prisoner of War and Civilian Internee WISP.

c. Guidance for unified and specified commanders in matters pertaining to Enemy Prisoner of War and Civilian Internee WISP.

2. Unified and specified commanders are responsible for all matters pertaining to Enemy Prisoner of War and Civilian Internee WISP in the area under their jurisdiction.

209

3. Prisoner of War WISP Detachments will be established, trained, and assigned to overseas area commands by the Department of the Army.

4. In areas where National WISP is operating, the Director of WISP, Office of WISP, will review communications to and from enemy prisoners of war and civilian internees in accordance with Armed Forces WISP regulations.

IX.   EFFECTIVE DATE AND IMPLEMENTATION

This Directive is effective immediately. Two (2) copies of each implementing document will be forwarded to the Assistant Secretary of Defense (Administration) within sixty (60) days.

-SIGNED-
Deputy Secretary of Defense

APPENDIX 5

Pgs. 212 thru 223

*AR 360–65
*OPNAV INST 5530.3A
*AFR 190–11

Army Regulation
No. 360–65
OPNAV Instruction
No. 5530.3A
Air Force Regulation
No. 190–11

DEPARTMENTS OF THE ARMY, THE NAVY,
AND THE AIR FORCE
Washington, D.C., *1 April 1966*

PUBLIC INFORMATION

ESTABLISHMENT AND CONDUCT OF FIELD PRESS CENSORSHIP IN COMBAT AREAS

*This publication supersedes AR 360–65/OPNAV Instr 5530.3/AFR 190–11, 15 August 1952.

TAGO 1574A—Apr. 200-474°—66

1

Section I. GENERAL

1. Purpose. This publication provides basic policies, procedures, and instructions for the establishment and operation of United States Armed Forces field press censorship (hereinafter referred to as Armed Forces field press censorship, or simply, as field press censorship) of news material (as hereinafter defined) subject to the jurisdiction of the Armed Forces of the United States in areas of operations and in other area commands as directed by competent authority. Additional guidance on field press censorship operations is contained in FM 45–25/OPNAVINST 5530.5/AFM 190–5 and TM 45–225/OPNAVINST 05530.7/AFM 190–6. Basic policies and instructions for the establishment and operation of civil censorship are contained in AR 380–83/OPNAVINST 5530.9/AFR 205–18; for Armed Forces censorship, in AR 380–200/OPNAVINST 5530.6A/AFR 205–30; and for enemy prisoner of war and civilian internee communications censorship, in AR 380–235/OPNAVINST 5530.11/AFR 205–9. The accreditation of correspondents, provision of communications facilities, and the internal dissemination of communications are additional matters not within the province of field press censorship.

2. Definitions. For the purpose of this publication the following definitions apply:

a. Area Armed Forces field press censorship organization. A group of persons assigned to an area command headquarters for the purpose of carrying out the field press censorship responsibility of the area commander.

b. Chief, Army, Navy, or Air Force field press censor. An officer appointed by the senior Army, Navy, or Air Force commander to exercise for him staff supervision over all field press censorship activities of his service in the force or area within his jurisdiction and to arrange for the provision of the field press censorship organization required therefor. Where appropriate, a Military Service chief field press censor may command the field press censorship organization of that Military Service. These officers should be especially qualified for and trained in field press censorship.

c. Chief field press censor. An officer appointed by the area or force commander to exercise for him staff coordination and supervision over and to implement all field press censorship in the area. A chief field press censor should be especially qualified for and experienced in field press censorship.

d. Correspondent. A journalist, press reporter, photographer, columnist, editor, publisher, radio or television reporter, commentator, cameraman, newsreel or other documentary picture production employee accredited to the Department of Defense and regularly engaged in the collection and dissemination of news to the public.

e. Director of Field Press Censorship. An officer appointed to serve in the Office of the Assistant Secretary of Defense, Public Affairs, ASD (PA), whose duties shall include the broad supervision and coordination of all field press censorship activities within the Armed Forces. He will specifically establish policies and promulgate directives that will promote uniformity of censorship in all areas. No command will issue subsequent directives or guidance at variance with those received from the Director of Field Press Censorship.

f. Espionage law stamp. A stamp bearing the following warning—

"This document contains information affecting the national defense of the United States within the meaning of the espionage laws, Title 18, U.S.C. sections 793 and 794; the transmission or the revelation of its contents in any manner to an unauthorized person is prohibited by law," which is placed in addition to the appropriate security classification, upon matter containing classified military information and delivered to persons other than those subject to the Uniform Code of Military Justice.

g. Field press censorship. The security review of news material subject to the jurisdiction of the Armed Forces of the United States, including all information or material intended for dissemination to the public.

h. Field press censorship detachment. A group of personnel responsible for field press censorship operations within an area or subdivision of an area or at a particular communications facility for the transmission of news material.

i. News material. All information and material, whether of fact or of opinion and whether visual or auditory, for dissemination to the public, including "letters to the editor" and service or business messages between a correspondent and his employer or agency.

j. Official military photographers. Members of photographic units of the Military Services will be considered official photographers when they are making photographic records for official purposes. When not acting in an official capacity, they are not considered official photographers and are therefore subject to Armed Forces censorship.

k. United States. The term "United States" includes the 50 States, the Commonwealth of Puerto Rico, Guam, the Virgin Islands, American Samoa and Swain's Island, the Canal Zone, the Trust Territories of the Pacific Islands, and any territory or area under the jurisdiction of the United States or which is committed to its control as administering authority by treaty or international agreement.

Note. Terms such as "commanding officer," "military," and "forces," shall apply equally to all Military Services.

3. Objectives. The twin objectives of Armed Forces field press censorship are to—

a. Insure the prompt release to the public of the maximum information consistent with security.

b. Prevent the disclosure of information which would assist the enemy.

4. Application. Field press censorship will be conducted in accordance with U.S. Armed Forces doctrine which will apply to the security review of news material subject to the jurisdiction of elements of the Armed Forces whether acting jointly or independently. The security review of news material subject to the jurisdiction of U.S. Armed Forces part of combined commands will be governed by procedure prescribed by the combined force commander so far as such procedure is in consonance with the principles set forth by the Department of Defense.

5. Staff responsibility. Staff supervision of field press censorship of the respective Military Services will be exercised through the following agencies:

a. Department of the Army. Chief of Information.

b. Department of the Navy. Chief of Information.

c. Department of the Air Force. Director of Information.

6. Command responsibility. *a.* The commander of a unified or specified oversea command will have overall responsibility for field press censorship within his command and the area under his jurisdiction (fig. 1).

b. The commander of a transient force will conform to the field press censorship regulations of the area which the force is transiting.

c. The commander of a unified or specified oversea command will be responsible for appointing a Chief Field Press Censor who will issue such directives as may be necessary for the operation of field press censorship within the area under his jurisdiction in consonance with directives issued by appropriate higher headquarters (para 4 above).

7. Establishment. Field press censorship may be established under the following conditions:

a. Within the United States. Upon declaration of war, or if the United States is attacked, or if the United States is believed about to be attacked, field press censorship may be established in the United States as directed by the Secretary of Defense with the approval of the President.

b. Outside the Continental United States. Field press censorship may be placed into effect immediately outside the Continental United States by a joint, specified, or other area commander of an area in which United States Armed Forces are operating, in the event of—

  (1) a declaration of war by the United States,

  (2) an armed attack upon the United States, its territories or possessions, or areas occupied or controlled by the United States,

  (3) an armed attack on the Armed Forces of the United States, or

  (4) the commitment to combat of Armed Forces of the United States as a separate force or as a part of a United Nations effort.

8. Scope of censorship. Field press censorship will be exercised over news material entering, leaving, or circulating within an area to the extent deemed by the area commander necessary for the maintenance of security. Normally, news material entering an area already will have been circulated widely and so have become available to the enemy, and hence no purpose would be served by stopping such news material. The strictness of field press censorship will depend primarily on the tactical situation in the area and contiguous territory. The information in news material is not associated necessarily with a specific military unit, and therefore may, in many instances, be published without compromise of security, whereas the same information cannot be permitted in the personal communications of individuals which might identify the unit concerned. When an area of active combat becomes inactive, immediate consideration will be given to the relaxation of field press censorship regulations. The complete abolition of field press censorship will not, however, be effected except as provided in paragraph 9.

9. Cessation. Wherever initiated or established, field press censorship will cease only upon the direction of the Secretary of Defense.

10. Operation. In combined operations, field press censorship policies will be coordinated at the highest practicable level. Optimum cooperation at all levels is essential to unity of effort and maintenance of security consistent with prompt release of news material. In joint commands, the area commander normally will cause field press censorship to be operated for the joint services as a single organization. In such cases, field press censorship personnel will be furnished by the respective Military Services on a basis prorated according to the activities of each of the Military Services. Close coordination among the Military Services will be established and maintained.

11. Jurisdiction. *a.* All news material of the following categories will be subject to field press censorship:

(1) News material including service or business messages from correspondents accredited to the area, force, or to lower echelons thereof.

(2) News material resulting from facilities granted by the area or force commander or by the headquarters of any lower echelons thereof.

(3) News material including "Letters to the Editor" prepared by persons in, attached to, serving with, or accompanying the Armed Forces of the United States.

(4) Civilian enterprise newspapers, news sheets, news bulletins, and similar publications published by civilians in the interests of persons in, attached to, serving with, or accompanying U.S. Armed Forces.

(5) Area type service and civilian welfare newspapers.

(6) Public information releases, productions, and material of all kinds including official photographic material for dissemination to the public.

(7) Psychological operations productions and material. Special cognizance will be taken of the requirement for expeditious review of such material. Normally, field press censors should be outposted at the points where such material is processed or transmitted. Where this is impracticable, authority to conduct the field press censorship review of such material may be delegated with the approval of the area or force commander to specifically designated psychological operations officers.

(8) Reports of the operations of the forces of the area or force commander (including foreign language material originating or published in liberated or occupied areas).

b.

(1) Responsibility for the maintenance of security in connection with material of the following categories is that of the officer responsible for the production and issuance thereof: Military Service and civilian welfare newspapers, news sheets, news bulletins, and similar unit and base publications other than area type Military Service and civilian welfare newspapers referred to in *a*(5) above.

(2) Officers responsible for the preparation and issuance of such material will maintain the closest liaison with field press censorship to insure conformity with this publication and any other pertinent field press censorship regulations and directives. Normally, such liaison will be accomplished by the submission of such material to field press censorship for review prior to issuance or publication.

c. The jurisdiction of field press censorship will not include the following:

(1) Personal communications subject to Armed Forces censorship under AR 380-200/OPNAVINST 5530.6A/AFR 205-30.

(2) Communications to prisoners of war and similar persons held by the Armed Forces

4

of the United States or its allies and from such persons held by the U.S. Armed Forces. Such material is a responsibility of the prisoner of war censorship authority established by the area commander.

(3) Communications to or from civilians not attached to, serving with, or accompanying the Armed Forces in territory occupied, controlled, or liberated by the U.S. Armed Forces. Such material is a responsibility of the established civil censorship authority of the area.

(4) News material (including foreign language material) originating or published in liberated or occupied areas other than psychological operations productions and material referred to in *a*(7) above, and reports of operations referred to in *a*(8) above. Such material is a responsibility of the established civil censorship authority of the area.

(5) Official military photographic material when in official channels, except that all such material for dissemination to the public will be submitted to field press censorship for review prior to the release thereof in accordance with *a*(6) above.

12. Field press censorship regulations. Wherever field press censorship is established, it will be conducted in accordance with this publication and such supplementary regulations and directives as the Department of Defense, the Departments of the Army, Navy, or Air Force, the area commander, or subordinate commanders delegated by the area commander, as appropriate, may issue. The area commander or delegated subordinate commanders will issue field press censorship directives based upon this publication and directives as applicable in the areas under their jurisdiction. Copies of such directives will be forward through normal command channels immediately upon promulgation to the Department of Defense, ATTN: Director of Field Press Censorship, and to the appropriate Military Departments.

13. Authorized channels for news material. *a.* Prior to transmittal or publication, all news material will be submitted for review to the appropriate field press censorship authority, as directed by the area or force commander.

b. Correspondents will employ only those communication facilities designated by the area or force commander.

c. All communication of news material, by whatever means, will be subject to field press censorship regulations. Material intended for publication including "Letters to the Editor" must be submitted to field press censorship. Correspondents may not include in personal correspondence any information which is intended directly or indirectly for use as source material or background information for publication in any manner. Any personal correspondence believed to contain such source or background information will be considered as business correspondence and submitted to field press censorship. When found in other channels, material intended for publication including "Letters to the Editor" and such correspondence believed to contain material intended for publication or source or background information will be referred by the appropriate Armed Forces censorship authority to field press censorship for examination.

d. All photographic news material will be processed within the area only in laboratory facilities approved by the area commander. In the event that laboratory facilities are available in the area, all such material and accompanying captions will be censored prior to shipment or transmission by radio or television. When laboratory facilities are not available, packages of negatives clearly labeled, "Negatives," and captions to accompany them will be shipped through such Armed Forces or other channels as are specified by the area commander to accomplish transmittal to the United States most expeditiously. These will be directed to the Assistant Secretary of Defense, Public Affairs, ASD(PA), Department of Defense, Washington, D.C., 20301, for delivery to the agency concerned for processing and submission to censorship prior to publication or release. The ASD(PA) may, in his discretion, direct that shipment be made directly to the agency concerned for processing and censorship prior to publication or release.

e. All news material based upon observations made while in an area subject to field press censorship regulation or pertaining to places visited therein, but prepared by a correspondent after his return to the United States will be subject to current field press censorship directives obtaining in such area and will be submitted prior to publication to the Office of the ASD(PA) for review.

f. In collaboration with the Armed Forces censorship authority of the area, field press censorship may conduct the censorship examination of communications carried by or included in the accompanied or unaccompanied personal effects of correspondents entering or leaving the area. The primary purpose of such examination will be to provide review by field press censorship personnel who are specially trained in the security review of news material, of the communications, notes, papers, diaries, sketches, and the like assembled by correspondents in their work. After censorship, such material will be packaged, sealed, and marked

on the outside with an Armed Forces area examiner stamp.

14. Field press censorship stamps. The stamps to be used in field press censorship will be uniform and designed as illustrated in figure 2. Stamps will be numbered serially in sets as indicated in figure 2 and will be procured and distributed by the respective Departments. The following blocks of numbers are allotted for identification of the Military Service possessing the stamp and the issuing Department:

a. Department of the Army---------------- 1-1000
b. Department of the Navy---------------- 1001-2000
c. Department of the Air Force----------- 2001-3000

Section II. SECURITY REVIEW OF NEWS MATERIAL

15. General. This section is applicable to all news material subject to field press censorship in an area where such censorship is in effect.

16. Basic procedures. *a. Rapid transmission.* The importance of speed in the handling of news material is emphasized. News material will be reviewed by field press censorship with the utmost dispatch. Release of the maximum of information consistent with security will be stressed. In doubtful instances, the need for security will have precedence over the need for speed in transmission. All submissions will be examined in the order of receipt by field press censorship.

b. Place of examination. Every effort will be made to conduct field press censorship at locations convenient to processing and transmission facilities. It is important that adequate space be provided for field press censorship activities, including the filing, logging, and censoring of submissions. Censorship should be accomplished in an material submitted by a given correspondent from area restricted from correspondents so as to protect competing news agencies.

c. Releasable information. The governing principle will be that the security review of news material will be accomplished within the shortest practicable time, and the maximum information released to the public consistent with denial of aid to the enemy. Following this principle, news material will be released unless it contains information requiring protection in the interests of national defense as defined by Executive Order 10501, 5 November 1953, and by implementing Department of Defense Instructions and Direc-

tives and Military Department regulations. It is emphasized that field press censorship is exercised for security only, and that news material will not be deleted or stopped on policy grounds. Censorship may not be used for the purpose of concealing administrative error or inefficiency, to prevent embarrassment, or to prevent release of official information which does not require protection in the interests of national defense.

d. Information of casualties and nonbattle dead, missing, and seriously ill. Information of casualties and nonbattle dead, missing, and seriously ill personnel of the Armed Forces of the United States and other persons for whom the Military Services render casualty reports will be released as soon as possible after official notification of the emergency addressee. Such information will be passed for publication by field press censorship upon the expiration of the period of time after the dispatch of official notification fixed by the Military Service concerned.

17. Organization. While, in principle, decentralization of field press censorship is undesirable from the points of view of both security and consistency, it is recognized that considerable decentralization will be required in order to provide speedy clearance of news material. Operating field press censorship installations will be located within the area of operations or other area at the facilities established for the transmission and processing of news material. Generally, transmission facilities and accompanying field press censorship installations will not be located forward of headquarters of field armies. The establishment of new installations or the inactivation of others always should be considered whenever changes in the situation with respect to transmission and processing facilities in an area occur. While security is the primary consideration in determining what information is to be released, provision for the speedy clearance of news material should always be the primary consideration in determining the location of field press censorship installations. Force or area commanders will, as the situation warrants, issue instructions through normal command channels delineating the responsibilities of subordinate commanders regarding appropriate policies and procedures for the processing of news submissions.

18. Responsibilities of chief field press censor. The chief field press censor will—

a. Coordinate and supervise the establishment of a field press censorship organization of sufficient size to effect the review of the maximum amount of news material which it is anticipated will require review and promulgate the necessary directives, field press censorship guidances, and administrative memoranda required to govern field press censorship activity and to maintain a uniform field press censorship policy within the area.

b. Allocate field press censorship detachments as required.

c. Be responsible for field press censorship in any case where news material cannot be conveniently dealt with by an out-posted field press censorship detachment.

d. Deal with points of doubt referred by outposted field press censorship detachments for determination.

e. Make provision for necessary liaison on censorship matters with other agencies in the military establishment, particularly the Armed Forces censorship authority, and with civil or military authorities of any allied or neutral government having jurisdiction over the area involved. In matters of primary importance, the Departments of the Army, the Navy, or the Air Force, as appropriate, should be made cognizant of such liaison especially when an allied or neutral government is involved.

19. Responsibility of chief Army, Navy, and Air Force field press censors. The duties of the chief Army, Navy, and Air Force field press censors are—

a. To supervise the establishment and operation of field press censorship pertaining to his respective Military Service.

b. Where appropriate, to command the field press censorship organization of his respective Military Service.

c. To prepare such reports on field press censorship operations or on information gained therefrom as are required by or would be helpful to the appropriate Department.

d. To provide for necessary instruction of field press censors under his supervision and for furnishing them with any information they may require for the proper performance of their duties.

20. Appointment of field press censors. *a. General.* Only commissioned officers of the respective Military Services are authorized to be appointed as field press censors. The area or force chief field press censor will assign an identifying number to each field press censor under his jurisdiction.

b. Qualifications. Field press censorship is an important aspect of the military public information function of assisting the public information media to inform the public. It is of the utmost importance that officers selected for this duty be chosen, not only on the basis of their experience and background in military security and military affairs, but also on the basis of an established background of knowledge and understanding of the vital need for getting news to the public and an understanding and sympathetic attitude toward the problems of correspondents. Personnel assigned to this duty should be mature officers with sufficient experience and background to appreciate the significance of military actions and preferably with experience in fields requiring the critical analysis of information.

21. Duties of field press censors. *a.* Each field press censor will perform field press censorship under the direction of the detachment chief field press censor.

b. Each field press censor will be responsible for a thorough knowledge of area field press censorship regulations and for proper and expeditious review of the news material he censors.

c. Field press censors any other persons who have access to news material will respect the property rights of each correspondent in the news material submitted by him and the confidential nature of the information which comes into their possession in the performance of their duties.

They will neither discuss nor disclose any such information in public or in private except when making a report in accordance with a lawful order, testifying or submitting evidence pursuant to the order of a duly constituted authority, or otherwise acting in the course of official business in matters pertaining to their office.

d. Neither the field press censor, nor any other person employed in field press censorship, will make any mark on or insert any writing in news material submitted to him for review except as specifically required in the performance of his duties. When authorized in advance in writing by a correspondent, field press censors may make minor insertions or substitute general designations for specific references to retain the continuity of thought in the submission.

22. Supplies and equipment. *a.* All field press censorship equipment and supplies (including stamps, knives or razor blades, field censorship DD forms, and any other supplies peculiar to censorship, which are necessary for the operation, and which are not produced in the field) will be requisitioned by, or by authority of, the area commander through area supply channels from the oversea supply division of the port of embarkation in the United States which is responsible for supplying the area.

b. Upon cessation of field press censorship, all stamps will be disposed of in accordance with instructions from the appropriate Department.

23. Field press censorship stamps. *a. Issue.* Sets of field press censorship stamps will be issued by, or by authority of, the area chief field press censor as required and will be issued only to, and used only by, personnel duty appointed to perform field press censorship.

b. Safeguarding. When such stamps are not in use by authorized personnel, they will be stored in a secure manner as determined by the senior field press censor of the installation. The loss, possible compromise, or unauthorized use thereof will be reported immediately to the area or force chief field press censor.

c. Transfer. When a set of stamps is transferred or surrendered by the field press censor to whom it was issued, a written acknowledgment signed by both parties to the transfer, or formal advice of the surrender, will be forwarded to the office of issue or record in the area.

d. Use.

(1) *General.* Under no circumstances will unexamined news material be stamped. A field press censor will place his identifying number and initials in the stamp imprint. The "Passed for publication," "Passed for publication as censored," "Not to be published until _____," and "No United States Army (Navy, Air Force) security" stamps should be used with blue or black ink; the "Not to be released" and "Not to be released before _____" stamps should be used with red ink.

(2) *Still pictures.* In censoring still pictures, only prints, not negatives, are stamped, and they are stamped on the back. If the caption is pasted or printed on the back of the print, the stamp should be placed so as to overlap parts of both print and caption. If the caption is on a separate sheet of paper, the stamp should be placed on both the caption and the reverse of the print.

24. Field press censorship forms. The following forms, when required, will be available through normal publications supply channels. If not so available, they will be produced locally.

a. DD Form 627 (U.S. Armed Forces Field Press Censorship Record of Submissions). Form used by logging clerk in handling of copy.

b. DD Form 628 (U.S. Armed Forces Field Press Censorship Log). Form used by field press censor in recording his handling of a submission.

25. Record of submissions. *a. When prepared.* A complete entry will be made with respect to all news material submitted for field press censorship.

b. How prepared.

(1) Full and accurate completion with respect to each submission of all data called for by this form is essential, because this record is the means by which the time taken by field press censorship in reviewing, and the disposition made of a particular submission can be traced.

(2) Appropriate entries will be made by the field press censorship logging clerk of the PIO copy room log number or other identifying number of the submission, name of correspondent and agency, na-

8

ture of submission, time in, time out,
action taken ("Passed," "Passed as censored," or "Stopped"), and name and
number of the censor who handled the
submission.

(3) Submission number and date time of
receipt will be recorded on copy submissions and marked in an appropriate place
on all other type submissions.

26. Log. *a. When prepared.* A log will be
prepared in every case by the field press censor
handling a submission.

b. How prepared.

(1) A full and accurate log with respect to
each submission is essential since this
form is one of the principal means by
which consistency and continuity of field
press censorship are achieved.

(2) Entries in logs will be brief and concise
and pertinent information will be clearly
stated. Whenever a field press censor
handles a submission, he will keep a separate log recording the source of the submission (author and agency); the nature
of the submission (e.g., photograph,
cable, telephone call, personal query,
etc.); the date, hour, and minute he received the copy; a brief description of the
subject matter of the submission; the
precise action he took, including a statement of the material or exact copy deleted
(if such copy is lengthy, a synopsis will
suffice), significant material passed which
will be helpful to other censors in
achieving consistency of censorship
action; the exact time of the completion
of the action and the submission number.

**27. Censorship of news material (other than
photographic, radio, or television).** *a. How
submitted.* News material, other than photographic, radio or television, will be submitted to
field press censorship in duplicate through the PIO
copy room or other authorized transmission
agency. Unless otherwise authorized, it will be
submitted in the English language. One copy will
be retained by field press censorship.

b. Action of field press censor.

(1) *News material to be transmitted by electrical means.* The field press censor will
review the submission in the light of current field press censorship guidance, de-

leting any information which is not
releasable by blue penciling same. Material of concern to a particular service
should be reviewed by a field press censor
of that service, and the "No United States
Army (Navy, or Air Force) security"
stamp employed to show that this has
been done. Upon completion of the review, the field press censor will conform
the duplicate of the submission and place
the appropriate stamp on the original and
duplicate. The original submission will
then be returned to the PIO copy room or
other authorized transmission agency.

(2) *Mailers.* News material going forward
by mail will be handled by the field press
censor in exactly the same manner as is
provided for material to be transmitted
by electrical means ((1) above), except
that information not releasable will be
removed physically from the original submission and indicated on the duplicate by
blue penciling. All excisions made in
the original submission will be destroyed
by burning.

c. Correspondents' file copies of submissions.
Correspondents will submit all copies of submissions to field press censorship and will not retain
copies thereof in their own files except as hereinafter provided. Correspondents who wish to
maintain a file of submissions will submit same in
triplicate. In such case the field press censor will,
in addition to the procedure outlined in *b*(1)
above, conform the triplicate of the submission and
place the appropriate stamp thereon. In the
event the submission is "Passed for publication,"
the triplicate will then be returned to the submitter. In the event the submission is "Passed for
publication as censored" the triplicate of the submission will be dealt with as submission going forward by mail (*b*(2) above) and then returned to
the submitter. In the case of stopped submissions
all copies of the submission will be retained by field
press censorship except as provided in paragraphs
30*a* and 31*a*. Upon request by field press censorship, correspondents will certify in writing that all
copies of a particular submission have been submitted to field press censorship.

28. Censorship of photographic material. *a.
Still photographs.*

(1) *How submitted.* Unless otherwise directed by the area chief field press censor,

two prints of still photographs will be submitted with captions. One print will be retained by field press censorship.

(2) *Action of field press censor.*

(a) The field press censor will review each photograph in the light of current field press censorship guidance. The print will be stamped as indicated in paragraph 23*d*(2). Required deletions will be indicated by red grease pencil. Deletions should not be made if the effect of the deletion is to focus attention on some new device or item of equipment which is classified. In such case the entire photograph should be stopped. Care should be exercised in stamping and initialing prints. Deep impressions readily show through and destroy the quality and usefulness of the print. Upon completion of his review, the field press censor will conform the two prints and place the appropriate stamp on them. One of the two prints submitted will then be returned to the submitter's approved laboratory which will, in the case of a photograph which has been "Passed for publication as censored," conform to the returned print in processing further prints so that the indicated nonreleasable material does not appear thereon. Responsibility for the making by his approved laboratory facility of the necessary alterations in the additional prints for publication is that of the submitter. In the case of a "Not to be released" photograph, the "Not to be released" print, properly stamped, will be returned to the submitter's approved laboratory facility for filing with the negative thereof as evidence of the field press censorship ruling thereon. Prints returned to the submitter's approved laboratory facility marked, "Passed for publication as censored" or "Not to be released" will be identified as security information by field press censorship and assigned an appropriate security classification. They will then be marked or stamped with such security classification in accordance with applicable security policies (AR 380–5, OPNAV Inst. 5510.1C, or AFR 205–1).

Such prints, together with the negatives thereof will be safeguarded by the submitter's approved laboratory accordingly. In such cases, where appropriate, field press censorship in addition to marking the returned print with the appropriate security classification will affix thereto the espionage law stamp.

(b) Prints going forward by mail will be handled by the field press censor in exactly the same manner as is provided for prints to be returned to the submitter's approved laboratory ((a) above) except that nonreleasable information will be removed physically from the print going forward and indicated on the field press censorship file print by red grease penciling. Minor deletions will be made on the print going forward by gently scratching out the nonreleasable information was a razor blade or other cutting instrument. In the case of larger deletions the emulsion containing the nonreleasable information should be cut out and then separated from the back of the print.

(c) Field press censors may require review of conformed prints.

b. Motion pictures.

(1) *How submitted.* Submission of motion picture material to field press censorship is by exhibition of a print of the film.

(2) *Action of field press censor.* The field press censor will tell the photographer or his representative what information must be deleted. These cuts will be noted by the field press censor and the photographer or his representative, and at the completion of the screening the items to be deleted from the footage will be listed and signed by the field press censor in duplicate. One copy becomes part of the permanent field press censorship log, and the other is used by the submitter's approved laboratory to make the required cuts in the prints of the film for release. The record of the cuts is classified security information and should be protected accordingly if transmitted with the film. Prints returned to the submitter's approved laboratory marked, "Passed for publication as censored" or "Not to be re-

leased," together with the negative thereof, will be identified as security information by field press censorship and assigned an appropriate security classification. They will then be marked or stamped with such security classification in accordance with applicable security policies and they will be safeguarded by the submitter's approved laboratory accordingly. Any material cut from a print or negative in order to produce a clear print for release will be destroyed by burning or safeguarded in accordance with applicable security policies. When appropriate, field press censorship, in addition to marking the returned print with the appropriate security classification, will affix thereto the espionage law stamp.

(3) Field press censors may require review of conformed prints prior to release.

29. Censorship of radio and television broadcasts. *a. Scripts.* Where a script is prepared in advance, the script will be submitted to field press censorship in duplicate and dealt with as provided in paragraphs 27*a* and *b*(1). In the case of a telecast from an area subject to the jurisdiction of field press censorship, all other aspects of the telecast will be dealt with as provided in *c* below.

b. Recordings. Submission of disc, tape, and wire recordings to field press censorship is by the playing of the material. The field press censor will specify which portions of the recording must be deleted. Required deletions will be accomplished during the review in order to remove the possibility of error and to maintain continuity in the recording.

c. Live broadcasts. Live radio and television broadcasts present special difficulties to field press censorship in the maintenance of security control and careful arrangements are required for their handling. Ordinarily, all news material intended for radio or television broadcast will first be taped and then submitted for censorship action. In the event this is not practicable, all participants will be briefed in advance on the security problems which may be encountered and the methods of avoiding them. The correspondent may be required to interrogate from a prepared script, relying on the other participants, guided by the briefing before the broadcast, to stay within security limits in their answers. In some cases it

may be advisable that arrangements be made for the field press censor to indicate by a prearranged sign whether or not a particular query may be answered so that if the information called for by the question is not releasable the interviewee can decline to answer the question. Provision will be made for a control switchoff so that the field press censor covering the performance can break the circuit if required in the event a participant inadvertently refers to classified information. Switch censorship is not a wholly effective safeguard since any breach of security usually would have occurred before the field press censor could switch off. Responsibility for security therefore must be assumed by the participants who will be so advised by the field press censor in charge. In live television broadcasts great care will be exercised to insure that nothing is included in picture or background which would constitute a violation of security. For security reasons, upon specific order of the area or force commander, the making of live radio or television broadcasts may be suspended in specified areas or for specific periods of time.

30. Security and publication delay. *a.* News material not releasable at the moment, but which later will be freely releasable, frequently is submitted to field press censorship. In such cases the field press censor will review the submission in the usual way, placing on it the "Passed for Publication" or "Passed for Publication as Censored" stamp, pending the release date. To avoid the possibility of the release of such material in advance of the security release time, he will simultaneously place across the face of the submission the Security Embargo stamp "Not to be released before ___ ____ " and insert the release date or prescheduled release time. Whenever the Security Embargo stamp is used, field press censorship will retain the submission until the specified time for release (para 23*d*(1)).

b. Publication delay. A publication delay is employed in situations where security does not forbid the *transmission* of news material, but the submission may not be *published* before a specified time. Illustrations of the employment of a publication delay are the lifting of a security classification on an item of equipment, coordinated by the appropriate Department so that correspondents in various localities are treated uniformly. Once it is determined that the security classification may be lifted, there may be no security bar to immediate transmission of news material about the equipment, but field press censorship, in order to lift the security restriction in a way which is fair to correspondents wherever located must require that the stories carry the slug, "Not to be published until _____." Similarly, the advance text of a speech or an announcement may be made available, and there may be no security objection to its transmittal before the speech is delivered or the announcement actually is made, so long as the text is not published prematurely. Whenever a publication delay is in effect, submissions are reviewed, stamped with both the censorship stamp and the publication delay stamp, "Not to be published until _____," and returned for transmittal in advance of the time indicated so long as the publication time is transmitted as an integral part of the text of the news material.

31. Disposition of stopped material. Certain news material submitted to field press censorship is not releasable at the moment but may be releasable at a future time. News material so stopped, including security embargoes, will be dealt with as follows:

a. News material to be transmitted by electrical means, mailers and scripts. Field press censorship will retain all copies of the submission. When authorized by the area chief field press censor, the original of a temporarily stopped submission, may, upon the request of the submitter therefor, for the purpose of expediting transmission upon later removal of classification, be returned to the submitter. In such case the submitter must be designated an official courier by appropriate authority for the purpose of resubmitting the particular news material to another field press censor. The official courier must resubmit the news material to a censor within a time limit determined by the appropriate authority to be reasonable and necessary under the circumstances of the particular case. Where appropriate, field press censorship will in such case, in addition to marking the submission with the appropriate security classification, affix thereto the espionage law stamp.

b. Photographic news material. One of the two prints submitted is returned properly stamped to the submitters' approved laboratory facility for file. Photographic news material is governed by considerations different from those applicable to material of the kind considered in *a* above. In accordance with paragraph 13*d*, within the area, photographic news material is processed only in laboratory facilities approved by the area commander. Where such material is "Passed for publication as censored," one of the two prints submitted must be returned by field press censorship to the submitter's approved laboratory facility for processing, so that the indicated nonreleasable information will not appear in further prints processed for publication. The submitter retains in the files of his approved laboratory facility the negative of all photographic news material taken by him, whether "Passed for publication as censored," or "Not to be released." "Not to be released" prints, as well as those "Passed for publication" or "Passed for publication as censored," properly stamped, are retained in such files as evidence of the field press censorship ruling thereon.

32. Information about field press censorship action. In all cases where extensive deletions must be made from a submission, the correspondent will be notified prior to the transmission of the story. If the correspondent cannot be located within a reasonable time, the submission should be given a final check and, if it still makes intelligible reading and its sense is not seriously altered, transmitted. Individual correspondents or agencies may desire and request that they be notified of all cuts before the copy is transmitted. Field press censorship will respect such requests. No addition will be made to the text of a submission without the express consent of the correspondent. Similarly, a correspondent will be notified when his submission must be held for release at a later date or is stopped.

Section III. TRAINING

33. Training of field press censors. Training of field press censorship personnel will be conducted under the supervision of the respective Departments at such locations as may be designated. So far as practicable, training will be conducted by the Military Services jointly and will include comprehensive instruction in the public information field, in forms of censorship operated by the military establishment, and in the operations of national censorship in the United States and by other governments. Field press censorship training will be directed toward the development of coordinated field press censorship teams for field operations. In time of war or emergency, such training will, if practicable, be conducted at places where press censorship is in effect and will include on-the-job training in press censorship.

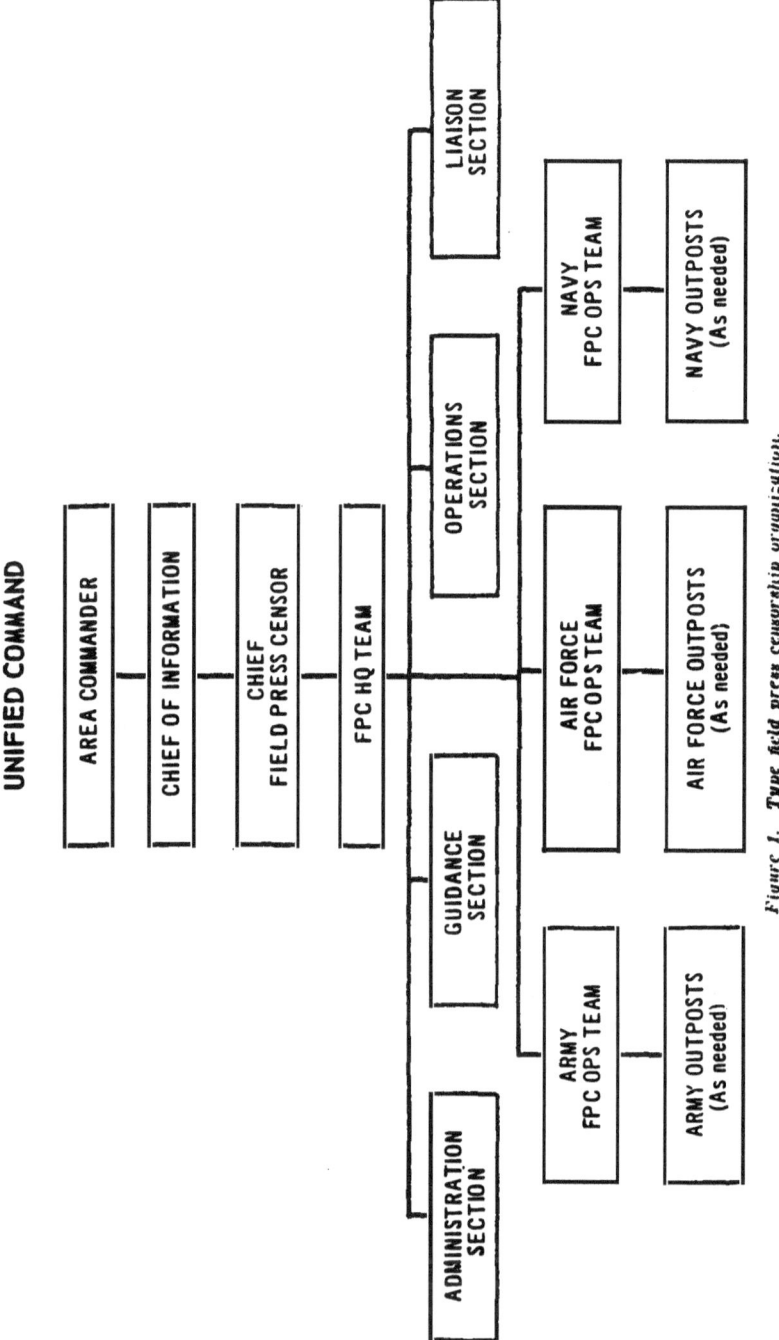

Figure 1. Type field press censorship organization.

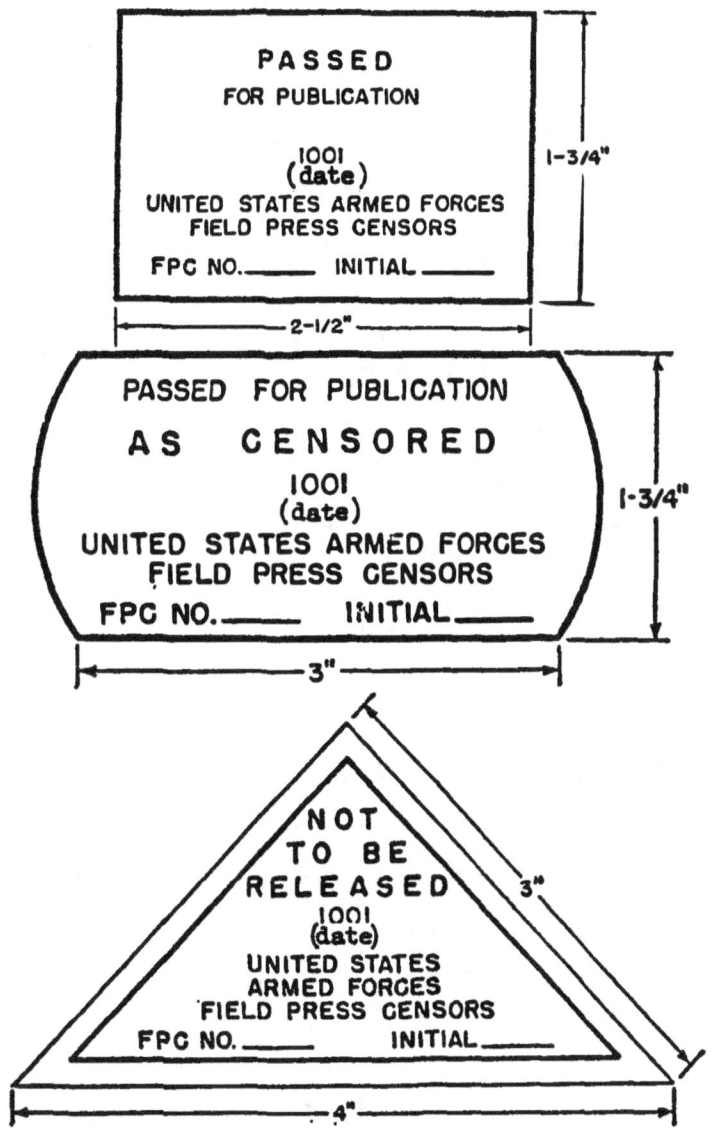

Figure 2. Field press censorship stamps.

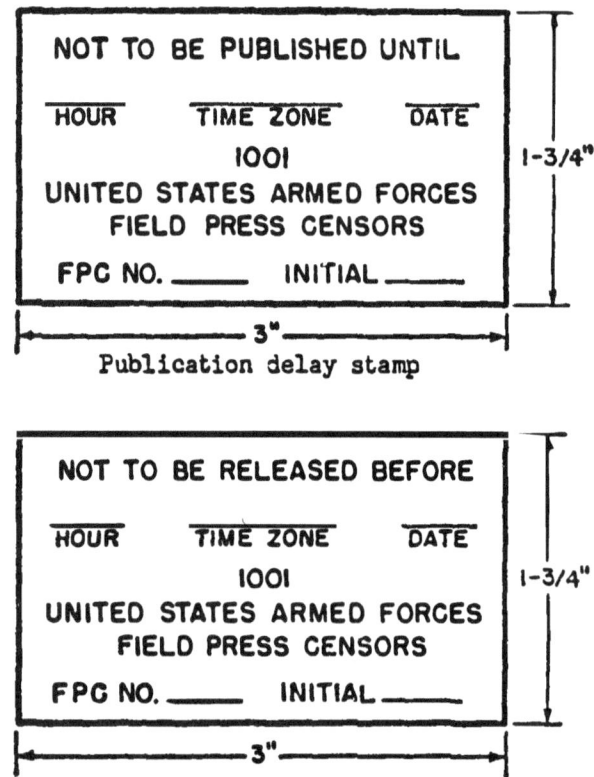

Figure 2. Field press censorship stamps—Continued

PUBLIC INFORMATION

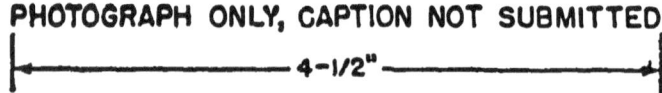

Figure 2. Field press censorship stamps—Continued

[CINFO]

By Order of the Secretaries of the Army, the Navy, and the Air Force:

HAROLD K. JOHNSON,
General, United States Army,
Chief of Staff.

Official:

J. C. LAMBERT,
Major General, United States Army,
The Adjutant General.

ROY S. BENSON,
Rear Admiral, United States Navy,
Assistant Vice Chief of Naval Operation
Director of Naval Administration.

J. P. McCONNELL,
General, U.S. Air Force,
Chief of Staff.

Official:

R. J. PUGH,
Colonel, USAF,
Director of Administrative Services.

Distribution:

Army:

Active Army: To be distributed in accordance with DA Form 12–9 requirements for Adm istration—C.

NG: None.

USAR: None.

Navy:

"All Ships and Stations," (less Marine Corps activities not having Navy personnel attache

Air Force:

S.

16

TAGO 15

BIBLIOGRAPHY

BOOKS

Adams, Valerie. *The Media in the Falkland Campaign.* New
    York: St. Martin's, 1986.

Adkin, Mark. *Urgent Fury--The Battle for Grenada.*
    Lexington, Mass.: Lexington Books, 1989.

Ambrose, Stephen E. *Eisenhower--Soldier, General of the
    Army, President-Elect 1890-1952.* New York: Simon and
    Schuster, 1983.

Andrews, J. Cutler. *The North Reports the Civil War.*
    Pittsburgh: University of Pittsburgh Press, 1955.

Andrews, J. Cutler. *The South Reports the Civil War.*
    Princeton: Princeton University Press, 1970.

Arno, Andrew and Wimal Dissanayako, eds. *News Media in
    National and International Conflict.* Boulder:
    Westview, 1984.

Bailyn, Bernard and John B. Hench, eds. *The Press and the
    American Revolution.* Worcester: American Antiquarian
    Society, 1980.

Barrett, Edward H. *Truth is Our Weapon.* New York: Funk &
    Wagnalls, 1953.

Beman, Lamar T., ed. *Censorship of Speech and the Press.*
    New York: Wilson, 1930.

Bigelow, Donald N. *William Conant Church and the Army and
    Navy Journal.* New York: Columbia University Press,
    1952.

Blount, James H. *The American Occupation of the
    Philippines 1898-1912.* New York: Putnam & Sons, 1912.

Bolger, Daniel P. *Americans at War 1975-1986, An Era of
    Violent Peace.* Novato, Calif.: Presidio, 1988.

Braestrop, Peter. *Battle Lines.* New York: Priority Press
    Publications, 1985.

Braestrop, Peter. *Big Story.* New Haven, Conn.: Yale
    University Press, 1978.

Brown, Charles H. *The Correspondents' War: Journalists in
    the Spanish American War.* New York: Charles Scribner's

Sons, 1967.

Bullard, F. Lauriston. *Famous War Correspondents*. Boston:
Little, Brown and Co., 1914.

Butcher, Captain Harry C., U.S. Naval Reserve. *My Three
Years with Eisenhower*. New York: Simon and Schuster,
1946.

Cadwallader, Sylvanus. *Three Years With Grant*. New York:
Alfred A. Knopf, 1956.

Cooper, Kent. *The Right to Know: An Exposition of the
Evils of News Suppression and Propaganda*. New York:
Farrar, Straus and Cudahy, 1956.

Cornesbie, Alfred E. *The Stars and Stripes*. Westport,
Conn.: Greenwood, 1984.

Corwin, Edward S. *Total War and the Constitution*.
Freeport, New York: Books for Libraries Press, 1970.

Crozier, Emmet. *Yankee Reporters 1861-1865*. New York:
Oxford University Press, 1956.

Crozier, Emmet. *American Reporters on the Western Front
1914-1918*. New York: Oxford University Press, 1959.

De Fleur, Melvin L. *Theories of Mass Communication*. New
York: David McKay, 1972.

Elsberg, John, ed. *American Military History*. Washington,
D.C.: Center of Military History, U.S. Army, 1989.

Emery, Edwin and Michael Emery. *The Press and America: An
Interpretative History*. 4th ed. Englewood Cliffs, NJ:
Prentice Hall, 1978.

Emery, Edwin and Michael Emery. *The Press and America: An
Interpretative History*. 5th ed. Englewood Cliffs, NJ:
Prentice Hall, 1984.

Fraenkel, Osmond K., ed. *Media and the First Amendment in
a Free Society*. Amherst: University of Massachusetts
Press, 1973.

Fussell, Paul. *Wartime--Understanding and Behavior in the
Second World War*. New York: Oxford University Press,
1989.

Gerald, J. Edward. *The Press and the Constitution: 1931-

1947. Gloucester: Peter Smith, 1968.

Halberstam, David. *The Best and the Brightest*. Greenwich,
    Conn.. Fawcett, 1973,

Hallin, Daniel C. *The Uncensored War*. New York: Oxford
    University Press, 1986.

Hammond, William M. *Public Affairs: The Military and the
    Media*. Washington, D.C.: U.S. Government Printing
    Office, 1988.

Higgins, Marguerite. *Our Vietnam Nightmare*. New York:
    Harper and Row, 1966.

Higgins, Marguerite. *War in Korea-The Report of A Woman
    Combat Correspondent*. Garden City, N.Y.: Doubleday,
    1951.

Hooper, Alan. *The Military and the Media*. Hants, England:
    Gower, 1982.

Hudson, Frederic. *Journalism in the United States From
    1690 to 1872*. New York: Harper & Brothers, 1873.

Kahn, E. J., Jr. *The Peculiar War-Impressions of a
    Reporter in Korea*. New York: Random House, 1952.

Knightley, Phillip. *The First Casualty*. New York:
    Harcourt, Brace, Jovanovich, 1976.

Koop, Theodore F. *Weapon of Silence*. Chicago: University
    of Chicago Press, 1946.

Langley, Lester D. *The Banana Wars-United States
    Intervention in the Caribbean 1898-1934*. Chicago:
    Dorsey Press, 1988.

Leckie, Robert. *The Wars of America*. New York: Harper and
    Row, 1981.

Lefever, Ernest W. *TV and National Defense*. Boston:
    Institute for American Strategy Press, 1974.

Levy, Leonard W., ed. *Freedom of the Press from Zenger to
    Jefferson*. Indianapolis: Bobbs-Merrill, 1966.

Lewinski, Jorge. *The Camera at War*. New York: Simon and
    Schuster, 1978.

McLuhan, Marshall. *Understanding Media: The Extensions of*

Man. New York: McGraw-Hill, 1966.

McMaster, John B. _Benjamin Franklin as a Man of Letters_.
    Boston: Houghton, Mifflin and Co., 1900.

Manchester, William. _American Caesar: Douglas MacArthur
    1880-1964_. New York: Dell, 1978.

Miller, Stuart C. _Benevolent Assimilation--The American
    Conquest of the Philippines, 1899-1903_. New Haven,
    Conn.: Yale University Press, 1982.

Millis, Walter. _Arms and Men: A Study in American
    Military History_. New York: Putnam, 1956.

Millis, Walter. _Road to War_. Boston: Houghton Mifflin,
    1935.

Mock, James R. _Censorship 1917_. Princeton, NJ: Princeton
    University Press, 1941.

Moeller, Susan D. _Shooting War_. New York: Basic Books,
    1989.

Morrison, David E. and Howard Tumber. _Journalists at War_.
    Beverly Hills: Sage, 1988.

Mott, Frank L. _American Journalism, A History: 1690-1960_.
    Toronto: MacMillan and Company, 1969.

Nacht, Michael. _Commercial Satellites and Crisis
    Decisions_. Washington, D.C.: University of Maryland
    Press, 1988.

Nelson, Harold L., ed. _Freedom of the Press from Hamilton
    to the Warren Court_. Indianapolis: Bobbs-Merrill,
    1967.

Nelson, Harold L., and Teeter, John L., Jr. _Law of Mass
    Communications_. 6th ed. New York: Foundation Press,
    1989.

Nichols, David, ed. _Ernie's War: The Best of Ernie Pyle's
    World War II Dispatches_. New York: Random House, 1986.

O'Brien, David M. _The Public's Right to Know: The Supreme
    Court and the First Amendment_. New York: Praeger,
    1981.

Pickett, Calder M. _Voices of the Past: Key Documents in
    the History of American Journalism_. Columbus, Ohio:

232

Grid, Inc., 1977.

Pyle, Ernie. *Here is Your War*. New York: Henry Holt & Co., 1945.

Quirk, Robert E. *An Affair of Honor: Woodrow Wilson and the Occupation of Vera Cruz*. New York: W. W. Norton & Co., 1962.

Remini, Robert V. *The Life of Andrew Jackson*. New York: Harper and Row, 1988.

Rice, Ronald E., ed. *The New Media: Communication, Research, and Technology*. Beverly Hills: Sage Publications, 1984.

Schlesinger, Arthur M. *The Rise of Modern America--1865-1951*. 4th ed. New York: MacMillan, 1951.

Seldes, George. *You Can't Print That! The Truth Behind the News 1918-1928*. New York: Payson & Clark, 1929.

Sims, Robert B. *The Pentagon Reporters*. Washington, D.C.: National Defense University, 1983.

Stein, M. L. *Under Fire--The Story of American War Correspondents*. New York: Julian Messner, 1968.

Summers, Col. Harry G., Jr., U.S. Army (Ret.). *On Strategy: The Vietnam War In Context*. Carlisle Barracks, Pa.: U.S. Army War College, 1982.

Summers, Robert E., ed. *Wartime Censorship of Press and Radio*. New York: H. W. Wilson, 1942.

Tansill, Charles C. *America Goes to War*. Boston: Little Brown & Company, 1942.

Tebbel, John. *The Compact History of the American Newspaper*. New York: Hawthorn, 1963.

Thompson, George R. and Dixie R. Harris. *The United States Army in World War II--The Technical Services--The Signal Corps: The Outcome (Mid-1943 Through 1945)*. Washington, D.C.: U.S. Government Printing Office, 1966.

Tussman, Joseph. *Government and the Mind*. New York: Oxford University Press, 1977.

Van Doren, Carl. *Benjamin Franklin*. New York: Viking

Press, 1938.

Voorhees, Lieutenant Colonel Melvin B., U.S. Army. *Korean
    Tales*. New York: Simon and Schuster, 1952.

Washburn, Patrick S. *A Question of Sedition: The Federal
    Government's Investigation of the Black Press During
    World War II*. New York: Oxford University Press, 1986.

Weisberger, Bernard A. *Reporters for the Union*. Boston:
    Little, Brown and Company, 1953.

Welch, Richard E., Jr. *Response to Imperialism--The United
    States and the Philippine-American War, 1899-1902*.
    Chapel Hill, NC: University of North Carolina Press,
    1979.

Westmoreland, General William C., U.S. Army. *A Soldier
    Reports*. New York: Dell, 1980.

Wiggins, James R. *Freedom or Secrecy*. New York: Oxford
    University Press, 1964.

Williams, David. *Not in the Public Interest: The Problem
    of Security in Democracy*. London: Hutchinson and
    Company, 1965.

Wise, David. *The Politics of Lying*. New York: Random
    House, 1973.

Wolff, Leon. *Little Brown Brothers--How the United States
    Purchased and Pacified the Philippine Islands at the
    Century's Turn*. New York: Doubleday, 1961.

Zumwalt, Ken. *The Stars and Stripes--World War II and the
    Early Years*. Austin: Eakin, 1989.

DOCUMENTS

Joint Chiefs of Staff. *The Joint Operation Planning
    System-Volume I Deliberate Planning Procedures (JCS
    Publication 5-02.1)*. Washington, D.C., 1988.

Joint Chiefs of Staff. *The Joint Operation Planning
    System- Volume I Deliberate Planning Procedures (SM362-
    84)*. Washington, D.C., 1984.

Joint Chiefs of Staff. *The Joint Operation Planning

234

System-Volume II Operation Plan Formats (JCS Publication 5-02.2 Draft). Washington, D.C., 1989.

Joint Chiefs of Staff. *The Joint Operation Planning System-Volume IV (Crisis Action Procedures) (JCS Publication 5-02.4)*. Washington, D.C., 1988.

Office of Technology Assessment, U.S. Congress. *Commercial Newsgathering from Space-A Technical Memorandum (OTA-TM-ISC-40)*. Washington, D.C.: U.S. Government Printing Office, 1987.

Office of the Assistant Secretary of Defense (Public Affairs). *Report by CJCS Media-Military Relations Panel (Sidle Panel)*. Washington, D.C.: U.S. Government Printing Office, 1984.

U.S. 201st Field Press Censorship Organization. *History of United States and Supreme Headquarters Allied Expeditionary Force Press Censorship in the European Theater of Operations, 1942-1945*. Paramus, NJ, 1953.

U.S. Department of Defense, "Defense 89 Almanac," Washington, D.C., September-October 1989.

U.S. Department of Defense, Defense Department Directives System Transmittal Cancellation Notice for Department of Defense Directive 5230.7, "Wartime Information Security Program (WISP)." Washington, D.C., 21 January 1987.

U.S. Department of Defense, Defense Information School, "Vietnam 10 Years Later." Fort Benjamin Harrison, Ind.: U.S. Government Printing Office, 1984.

U.S. Department of Defense. "Principles of Information." Secretary of Defense Caspar Weinberger. Washington, D.C., undated.

U.S. Department of Defense. *Wartime Information Security Program (WISP) (Department of Defense Directive 5230.7)*. Washington, D.C., with changes through 21 May 1971.

U.S. Department of the Army. *Army Information Officers' Guide (Department of the Army Pamphlet 360-5)*. Washington, D.C., 1968.

U.S. Department of the Army. *Communications-Electronics Fundamentals: Transmission Lines, Wave Propagation, and Antennas (Field Manual 11-64)*. Washington, D.C., 1985.

U.S. Department of the Army. *History of Military Mobilization in the United States Army 1775-1945 (Department of the Army Pamphlet 20-212)*. Washington, D.C., November 1954.

U.S. Department of the Army. *Public Affairs (Field Manual 46-1)* Washington, D.C., 1986.

U.S. Department of the Army, Department of the Navy, Department of the Air Force. *Public Information: Establishment and Conduct of Field Press Censorship in Combat Areas (Army Regulation 360-65, Operational Naval Instruction 5530.3A, Air Force Regulation 190-11)*. Washington, D.C., 1 April 1966.

U.S. Military Assistance Command, Vietnam. *Public Information Policies and Procedures (Military Assistance Command-Vietnam Directive 360-1)*. Saigon, 1967.

U.S. War Department. *Annual Report of the War Department for the Fiscal Year Ending June 30, 1898. Report of the Chiefs of Bureaus*. Washington, D.C.: U.S. Government Printing Office, 1898.

U.S. War Department. *Annual Report of the War Department for the Fiscal Year Ending June 30, 1899. Report of the Chiefs of Bureaus*. Washington, D.C.: U.S. Government Printing Office, 1899.

NEWSPAPERS

Brugioni, D. A. "Satellite Images on TV: The Camera Can Lie." *Washington Post*, 14 December 1986, p. H1.

Greider, William. "The Press as Adversary." *Washington Post*, 27 June 1971, p. B1.

Harwoody Richard. "The Military's Bogus Enemy." *Washington Post*, 11 March 1984, p. C5.

Lewis, Flora. "The Duty to Publish." *The New York Times*, 29 September 1987, p. A35.

Middleton, Drew. "Vietnam and the Military Mind." *The New York Times Magazine*, Jan. 10, 1982, p. 34.

"News Media Warned on Censorship Rules." *The Washington Post*, 13 August 1965, p. A9.

"Parents See G.I. Son Wounded on TV." *The New York Times*, 12 May 1967, p. 3.

Robinson, Walter V. "Journalists Constrained by Pentagon." *The Boston Globe*, 25 December 1989, p. 3.

"U.S. Reporter in Vietnam is Suspended for a Month." *The New York Times*, 1 February 1966, p. 14.

PERIODICALS

"Armed Forces Communications and Electronics Association Sustaining and Group Member Capabilities Directory-- Individual Company Listing 1989." *Signal* 43, No. 6 (February 1989): 177-358.

Baker, Capt. Brent, U.S. Navy. "Wanted: A Professional Press." *Proceedings*, Vol. 110/7/977 (July 1984): pp. 74-77.

Bennett, Tamara. "SATCOM Atop Everest." reprint from *Satellite Comunications Magazine*, Fall 1987.

Boomer, Brig. Gen. Walter E., U.S. Marine Corps. "Censorship of the Press." *Marine Corps Gazette* 72, No. 1 (January 1988): 18-19.

Brender, Mark E. "High Resolution Remote Sensing by the News Media." *Technology in Society* 2, No. 1 (1989): 89-98.

Budahan, P.J. "A War of Words." *Army Times* 50, No. 26 (February 5, 1990): 39-50.

Cleary, Col. Thomas J., Jr., U.S. Army. "Aid and Comfort to the Enemy." *Military Review* 48, No. 8 (August 1988): 51-55.

Doerner, William R. "Lead-Pipe Politics." *Time* 133, No. 21 (22 May 1989): 40-43.

Dwan, Col. John F., U.S. Marine Corps. "The Public Has a Right to Know." *Marine Corps Gazette* 72, No. 1 (January 1988): 19-20.

Eberhard, Col. Wallace B., U.S. Army. "A Familiar Refrain but Slightly Out of Tune." *Military Review* 67, No. 2 (February 1987): 71-84.

Eberhard, Lt. Col. Wallace B., U.S. Army. "From Balloon Bombs to H-Bombs." *Military Review* 59, No. 2 (February 1981): pp. 2-9.

Foisie, Jack. "My Third War." *Army*, 15, No. 15 (October 1965): pp. 31-34.

Garneau, George. "Military Press Pool Misses Most of the Action." *Editor & Publisher*, 6 January 1990, pp. 4, 84.

Halloran, Richard. "Soldiers and Scribblers: A Common Mission." *Parameters* 17, No. 1 (Spring 1987): pp 14-19.

Hammond, William M. "Military and the Media in Vietnam." *Army Public Affairs Monthly Update*, No. 90-6 (March 1990), pp. 10-13.

Hayward, Vice Adm. John T., U.S. Navy (Ret). "Military Responsibility and Freedom." *Strategic Review* 1, No. 3 (Fall 1973): 46-50.

Hofstetter, C. Richard and David W. Moore. "Watching TV News and Supporting the Military: A Surprising Impact of the News Media." *Armed Forces and Society* 5, No. 2 (Winter 1979): 261-269.

Howell, Maj. Cass D., U.S. Marine Corps. "War, Television and Public Opinion." *Military Review* 67, No. 2 (February 1987): 71-79.

Jamieson, John. "Censorship and the Soldier." *Public Opinion Quarterly* 2, No. 3 (Fall 1947): 367-384.

Kennedy, Col. William V., U.S. Army. "It Takes More Than Talent to Cover a War." *Army* 28, No. 7 (July 1978): 23-26.

Kittredge, Capt. Tracy B., U.S. Navy. "A Military Danger--The Revelation of Secret Strategic Plans." *Proceedings* 81, No. 7 (July 1955): 731-743.

Kiernan, Maj. David R. "The Case for Censorship." *Army* 33, No. 3 (March 1983): 22-24.

Koop, Theodore F. "We Need to Know." *Air Force* 38, No. 10

(October 1955): 46-50.

McKenzie, Richard. "The High Cost of Free Speech."
    National Review, 5 September 1983, 1063-1068.

Marshall, Eliot. "A Spy Satellite for the Press?" *Signal*,
    42, Number 9 (May 1988): 55-58.

Mead, Brig. Gen. James M., U.S. Marine Corps. "The MAU
    Meets the Press." *Marine Corps Gazette* 71, No. 9
    (September 1987): 19-21.

Migdail, Carl J. "A Perspective of the Military and the
    Media." *Naval War College Review* 28, No. 3 (Winter
    1976): 2-9.

Mock, James R., George Creel, Neville Miller, Zechariah
    Chafee, Jr., Ralph Casey, and Arthur Krock. "The
    Limits of Censorship: A Symposium." *Public Opinion
    Quarterly*, Spring 1942, 3-26.

Moon, Col. Gordon A. II. "Military Security vs. the Right
    to Know." *Army* 18, No. 7 (July 1968): 22-66.

Moon, Col. Gordon A. II. "The Right to Know." *Army* 16,
    No. 11 (November 1966): 47-50.

Newton, Ray. "Roles, Rights and Responsibilities: Who
    Should the Media Serve?" *The National Forum* 68, No. 4
    (Fall 1987): 2-4.

Norman, Lloyd. "The Love-Hate Affair Between the Pentagon
    and the Press." *Army* 30, No. 2 (February 1980): 14-20.

Pontuso, James F. "Combat and the Media: The Right to Know
    Versus the Right to Win." *Strategic Review* 18, No. 1
    (Winter 1990): 49-60.

Price, Byron. "Governmental Censorship in Wartime."
    American Political Science Review 36, No. 5 (October
    1942): 837-849.

"Realtime Video Compression." *PC Week*, 6 March 1989, p.
    69.

Reed, Fred. "Why the Media's Military Coverage Misses the
    Mark." *National Review*, 13 December 1985, 32-35.

Rinaldo, Lt. Col. Richard J., U.S. Army. "The Tenth Prin-
    ciple of War." *Military Review* 67, No. 10 (October
    1987): 55-62.

Rusher, William A. "The Media and Our Next Intervention: A
    Scenario." *Parameters* 18, No. 3 (September 1988): 6-
    15.

Say, Commander Harold B., U.S. Naval Reserve. "Censorship
    and Security." *Proceedings* 79, No. 2 (February 1953):
    135-141.

Scott-Barrett, D. W. "The Media and the Armed Services."
    Military Review 52, No. 4 (April 1972): 62-76.

Sheehan, Neil. "The Press and the Pentagon Papers." *Naval
    War College Review* 24, No. 6 (February 1972): 8-12.

Sidle, Maj. Gen. Winant, USA Ret. "The Military and the
    Press: Is the Breach Worth Mending?" *Army* 35, No. 5
    (May 1985): 22-32.

Sidle, Maj. Gen. Winant, USA Ret. "The Public's Right to
    Know." *Proceedings* 111/7/989 (July 1985): 37-44.

Smith, Lt. J. Morgan, USN. "Wanted: A Responsible Free
    Press." *Proceedings* 110/7/977 (July 1984): 77-85.

Smolowe, Jill. "Is Panama Worth the Agony?" *Time* 133, No.
    21 (22 May 1989): 44-49.

Summers, Col. Harry G., Jr., USA Ret. "Western Media and
    Recent Wars." *Military Review* 68, No. 5 (May 1986): 4-
    17.

Toole, Rear Adm. Wycliffe D., Jr., U.S. Navy. "Military
    Cover and Deception vs. Freedom of Information."
    Proceedings 101, No. 12 (December 1975): 18-25.

Upchurch, Col. Richard L., USMC. "Wanted: A Free Press."
    Proceedings 110/7/977 (July 1984): 68-74.

Van Voorst, Bruce. "How Reporters Missed the War." *Time*
    134, No. 2 (8 January 1990): 61.

"VIASAT's Portable Satellite Terminal."
    Telecommunications, July 1989, pp. 68-69.

Webb, James H., Jr. "The Military and the Media." *Marine
    Corps Gazette* 68, no. 11 (Nov. 1984): 30-37.

Weinberger, Caspar W. "The Delicate Balance Between a Free
    Press and National Security." *Defense 85* October 1985,
    2-7.

Willey, Maj. Barry E., U.S. Army. "Military Media
Relations Come of Age." *Parameters* 19, No. 1 (March
1989): 76-84.

Young, David M. "Security and the Right to Know."
Military Review 44, No. 8 (August 1964): 46-53.

Zoll, Donald A. "The Press and the Military: Some Thoughts
After Grenada." *Parameters* 14, No. 1 (Spring 1984):
26-34.

Zorthian, Barry. "The Role of the Communications Media in
a Democratic Society." *Naval War College Review* 24,
No. 6 (February 1972): 1-7.

Zuckerman, Laurence. "Sticky Issues in Gumshoe
Journalism." *Time* 8 August 1988, 72.

UNPUBLISHED SOURCES

Angelle, Maj. Alexander, U.S. Army. "U.S. Armed Forces
Public Affairs Roles in Low Intensity Conflict."
Unpublished Report, U.S. Army-Air Force Center *for Low*
Intensity Conflict, Langley Air Force Base, Va., 1988.

Cecil, Kelly and Mark Sullivan. "Media War Coverage and
Pentagon Policy." Unpublished policy analysis.
Cambridge, Mass., 1989.

Coleman, Lt. Col. Thomas L., Jr., U.S. Army. "The News
Media: Should They Play a Role in Crisis Management?"
Unpublished student paper, U.S. Army War College,
Carlisle Barracks, Pa., 1989.

Dolan, Lt. Col. Raymond J., U.S. Army. "Crisis Decision-
Making: The Impact of Commercial Satellites on the
Media, Military and National Leaders." Unpublished
student paper, U.S. Army War College, Carlisle
Barracks, Pa., 1989.

Dye, Lt. Col. John W., III, U.S. Army. "Censorship: An Old
Concept With New Problems." Unpublished student
thesis, U.S. Army War College, Carlisle Barracks, Pa.,
1987.

Gabriel, Capt. Peter. H., U.S. Army. "A Pilot Study of
Press-Military Relationships in the Aftermath of

Grenada.˙ Unpublished Report, U.S. Army Military
    Personnel Center, Alexandria, Va., 1985.

Gibbs, Col. Richard F., U.S. Air Force, and Freeman,
    Commander Linus W., U.S. Navy. ˙Censorship of the
    Press.˙ Unpublished monograph, U.S. Army War College,
    Carlisle Barracks, Pa., 1972.

Grossman, Patricia A. ˙The Future of Field Press
    Censorship: Is There One?˙ Unpublished student paper,
    U.S. Army War College, Carlisle Barracks, Pa., 1989.

Hoffman, Fred. ˙Report on the Press Pool - Operation *Just
    Cause*.˙ Unpublished report to the Assistant Secretary
    of Defense (Public Affairs), Washington, D.C., March
    1990.

Holk, Richard P. ˙Print Coverage of Military Conflict: The
    Los Angeles Times and the Vietnam War (A Content
    Analysis, 1964-1972).˙ Unpublished student thesis,
    California State University, Fullerton, Cal., 1979.

Humphries, Lt. Comdr. Arthur A., U.S. Navy. ˙Falklands War
    Public Affairs Analysis.˙ Unpublished research paper,
    U.S. Naval War College, Newport, RI, 1983.

Jefferson, Thomas, to Elbridge Gerry, 26 January 1799,
    The Writings of Thomas Jefferson, Thomas Jefferson
    Memorial Association Washington, 1904, Vol 10, p. 83.

Lindstrom, Fred B. ˙The Military Mind and the Soldier
    Press.˙ Unpublished student dissertation. University
    of Chicago, Chicago, Ill., 1950.

McCall, Col. Craig C., U.S. Air Force. ˙Influence of the
    News Media on the Armed Forces--Southeast Asia.˙
    Unpublished student paper. U.S. Air Force Air War
    College, Maxwell Air Force Base, AL, 1971.

Mander, Mary S. ˙Pen and Sword: A Cultural History of the
    American War Correspondent: 1895-1945.˙ Unpublished
    student thesis. University of Illinois, Urbana, 1970.

Miller, Maj. Billy F., U.S. Army. ˙Press Reporting:
    Prejudicial to Counterinsurgency Efforts?˙ Unpublished
    student paper, U.S. Army Command and General Staff
    College, Fort Leavenworth, Kans., 1971.

Mitchell, Maj. Michael C., U.S. Marine Corps. ˙Public
    Affairs as a Force Multiplier.˙ Unpublished student
    paper, U.S. Naval War College, Newport, RI, 1989.

Monroe, Col. Keith L., U.S. Army. "National Security
     versus the Fourth Estate." Unpublished student thesis,
     U.S. Army War College, Carlisle Barracks, Pa., 1968.

Office of the Deputy Chief Signal Officer, Supreme
     Headquarters Allied Expeditionary Force. "Press
     Communications." Letter to Chief Signal Officer, War
     Department, France, 1944.

Pike, Maj. T. E., U.S. Army. "Pragmatism: Its Effects on
     Civil Liberties During World War I." Unpublished
     student paper. U.S. Army Command and General Staff
     College, Fort Leavenworth, Kans., 1972.

Porter, Col. Tim L., U.S. Army. "Whither the War
     Correspondent?" Unpublished student thesis, U.S. Army
     War College, Carlisle Barracks, Pa., 1989.

Rixon, Maj. Malcolm D., U.S. Army. "Field Press
     Censorship." Unpublished student paper. Fort
     Leavenworth, Kans., 1965.

Rowland, Capt. Marianne. F., U.S. Army. "Media Access and
     War Reporting." Unpublished student thesis, U.S. Army
     Military Personnel Center, Alexandria, Va., 1985.

Scharnberg, Lt. Col. George R., U.S. Marine Corps. "The
     'Maximum Candor' Policy--Its Impact on Military-News
     Media Relationships." Unpublished student thesis, U.S.
     Army War College, Carlisle Barracks, Pa., 1969.

Sharpe, Lt. Col. Gerald. W., U.S. Army. "Army/Media
     Conflict: Origins, Development and Recommendations."
     Unpublished student thesis, U.S. Army War College,
     Carlisle Barracks, Pa., 1986.

Simpson, Lt. Col. Arthur. J., Jr., U.S. Army. "Wartime
     Public Media Censorship." Unpublished student thesis,
     U.S. Army War College, Carlisle Barracks, Pa., 1971.

U.S. Army War College Strategic Studies Institute. "Press
     Coverage of the Vietnam War: The Third View."
     Unpublished Study Group Report, U.S. Army War College,
     Carlisle Barracks, Pa., 1979.

U.S. Department of Defense. "DOD National Media Pool Alert
     Procedures for Bureau Chiefs," Washington, D.C., 5
     January 1990.

U.S. Department of Defense. DOD National Media Pool

243

Operational Procedures. Washington, D.C., 24 March 1989.

U.S. Department of Defense. Assistant Secretary of Defense (Public Affairs) message to all Department of Defense Public Affairs Activities. "Media Pool No. 3 After Action Report - Kernel Usher 86-I." Washington, D.C., 2 January 1986.

U.S. Department of Defense. Assistant Secretary of Defense (Public Affairs) message to all Department of Defense Public Affairs Activities. "Media Pool No. 4 After Action Report." Washington, D.C., 14 August 1986.

U.S. Department of Defense. Assistant Secretary of Defense (Public Affairs) message to all Department of Defense Public Affairs Activities. "Media Pool No. 5 After Action Report - Honduras." Washington, D.C., 19 February 1987.

U.S. Department of Defense. Assistant Secretary of Defense (Public Affairs) message to all Department of Defense Public Affairs Activities. "Media Pool No. 9 After Action Report/Recap of Media Pools." Washington, D.C., 30 December 1988.

U.S. Department of Defense. Assistant Secretary of Defense (Public Affairs) message to all Department of Defense Public Affairs Activities. "Public Affairs: Media Pool - After Action Report." Washington, D.C., 7 October 1985.

U.S. Department of Defense. Assistant Secretary of Defense (Public Affairs) message to all Department of Defense Public Affairs Activities. "Public Affairs: Media Pool - Universal Trek 85." Washington, D.C., 17 May 1985.